Junior high is a critical period in life. It is a time of rapid and often awkward development. At this point in children's lives their minds, moods, bodies, attitudes, and emotions are in a state of instability and erratic, uneven transformation. You can help your junior-high-aged child make adjustments during this time—and find peace of mind for yourself—if you know what to expect. In When Junior Highs Invade Your Home, *Cliff Schimmels familiarizes you with the day-to-day experiences and behavior of junior-high schoolers by offering you glimpses of them in specific situations and circumstances. You'll see that many problems which originate in school spill over into the home and other areas of the junior-higher's life. In clear, concise language, Dr. Schimmels employs sound biblical principles and offers helpful insight for dealing with the problems that arise when a junior high invades your home.*

When Junior Highs Invade Your Home

Cliff Schimmels

Power Books

Fleming H. Revell Company
Old Tappan, New Jersey

Library of Congress Cataloging in Publication Data

Schimmels, Cliff.
 When junior highs invade your home.

 1. Junior high school students—United States—Attitudes—Case
studies. 2. Junior high school students—United States—Social condi-
tions—Case studies. 3. Adolescence—Case studies. I. Title.
LC208.4.S34 1984   373.18   83-21306
ISBN 0-8007-5144-2 (pbk.)

Contents

With Thanks

One winter night I persuaded my best friend to go jogging with me. He skidded on the ice, fell, and broke his arm. After looking at that cast for several months, I promised myself not to ask him for any more favors.

But when I decided to write this book, I had to swallow that promise because he is the standard for junior high teachers. More than that, he is an expert on that age. But he is more than an expert on junior highers. He is also their friend, counselor, consultant, and model for a consistent, understanding adult.

Throughout my writing, I have depended on him for advice, details, stories, verification, and encouragement. But in the process, I gained more. As we spent time together, I suddenly realized that here is one man who spends every day with junior high people, and he is having a blast. And through his enthusiasm, I remembered how much I enjoy—yes, in fact love—those people who make up that wild, wonderful population segment we call junior highers. I pray that shows throughout the book.

Thanks, Robb Cooper, for your help and your friendship—and thanks especially for the vision.

We'll jog and talk about it—as soon as your arm heals.

1
A Hurricane Named Sherri

"Does she really hate me?"

Sherri was sick and missed the constitution test. In our school, that is a big deal. The constitution test is one of the biggest academic happenings of the year. It is one of those grade-level bench marks that students encounter all through the schooling process.

People in first grade learn to read; people in third grade learn to write cursive; people in fifth grade learn to add fractions; and, in our state (as well as several others), people in eighth grade study the constitution and take a big test. It is just one of those tasks assigned to a certain level of development. But in the case of the eighth grader, it is rather specific. If people are naturally curious or have pushy parents (or older siblings) they may learn to read before the first grade or learn to write cursive before the third grade but very few people ever study the constitution before the eighth grade. That is an activity that comes on schedule—at least in our school.

But Sherri was sick and missed it. The next day, we discussed a make-up time and agreed on Thursday afternoon right after school.

When the time came, I was ready with the make-up test all prepared. I don't forget things like that. I may not remember my wife's birthday, and I may walk home with the car still in the school parking lot, but I don't forget make-up tests.

But just as the bell rang to dismiss school, I got a note telling me to come downstairs for a telephone call. It was one of those calls from the district office; they were trying to arrange a committee meeting. I had to check my calendar for open dates. The people on the other end checked their calendars; then we shuffled and bargained. Finally, twenty minutes later, we came up with a date for the meeting, and I rushed back up to my classroom.

There sat Sherri just about to boil over. I tried explaining and apologizing at the same time, but neither worked. The eruption came with me standing right in the middle of its wake.

Her mother was coming in *ten* minutes. She just *had* to go to town today to buy some new cheerleader shoes. There was a game tomorrow, and the cheerleaders were going to wear uniforms all day. She had been there when I asked her to be. She had studied for the stupid old test the night before. She had worried about it all day long. She had better things to do with her time than sit in that stupid old room and wait for me to talk on the phone. She didn't have time to take that stupid old test. She just might *never* take it. She didn't care if she *did* flunk eighth grade. It was all my fault anyway. And she wasn't mad, and those weren't tears flowing down her cheek. And she was just going to leave, and there wasn't anything I could do about it.

With that announcement, she shut her books, got up, stormed out of the room with the grace of a hippopotamus, and slammed the door, jarring the tranquility of the then empty building and my soul.

I guess I have been an adult too long to take such things as that in stride. I felt terrible about the incident. All through the evening and night I felt terrible. Not even the funniest rerun of "M*A*S*H" could shake me loose from my concern. All night long I tossed and tumbled. I could not forget that girl in her misery.

Actually, I knew she was right. We had made an agreement, and I had not kept my word. I should have been there.

But how often am *I* kept waiting twenty minutes? I wait that long for a doctor's appointment. I wait that long to get in to see the principal, even when I have an urgent matter. And I don't act that violently. I may feel like it, but I don't act that way.

I felt myself caught between being angry and being sympathetic about her hurt feelings. And underlying all that was my own sense of guilt, knowing that if I had been on time, none of it would have happened.

I didn't want to go back to school the next day. I had twenty good relationships with eighth graders, but that one bad one was enough to sour the whole day. I didn't know how to face Sherri, and I didn't know how Sherri would face me. I dreaded the tension that would permeate the atmosphere of the whole class. But obedient to duty, I plodded back.

Before the beginning of the first period, I was standing outside the door to my room watching the half-children/half-adults scamper to class. This is a common ritual for junior high teachers. They are asked to stand outside their doors in between classes. They are to keep people from running in the hall. They are to keep boys from punching boys they don't like and girls they do. They are to watch for drug deals going down.

Just as I had lost myself in the activity of watching and had almost stopped dreading what was to come, a voice in the proximity of my right elbow said, "Mr. Schimmels." I turned and looked into that shining, beaming, sparkling face that belonged to Sherri. "Mr. Schimmels," she said with tones dripping straight from the beehive, "are you mad at me?"

* * *

Welcome to the wonderful world of junior high, middle school, young adolescence, or whatever it is you call those frantic, fruitful, frightful years that engulf people between the ages of twelve and fifteen.

As you can see, it is a world of extremes—extremes of emotions and moods, of sizes and shapes, of dreads and desires, of aims and ambitions. These years represent one of the most exciting and trying spans of life—both for the people caught in the period and for the people who inherit the job of helping them through it.

Since you are reading this book, I assume you are one of the latter—someone who has a special interest in helping a special person through this period of extremes and adjustments. In other words, I assume you are a parent of a junior-high-age child, and you are reading this book because you want to know how to do your job well. Perhaps you have a specific problem for which you need an answer, or perhaps you are just a bit frightened by the whole enterprise. Or perhaps you are just looking for confirmation of what you are already doing. Regardless of your motivation for reading it, I really want this book to help you.

If this were a typical how-to book, I would respond to your needs by simply developing a list of dependable generalities pertaining to junior-high-age people and then making some specific suggestions about how you should respond to these general needs and moods. Then you could apply the salve to the sore and everybody—you, your child, and I— could all go away content that we had done our jobs.

But this isn't a typical how-to book, because we are not talking about *typical* people. There is simply not such an animal as the typical junior high person. Everyone is different and everyone changes every day.

As a parent, particularly if you have more than one child, you have probably already come to appreciate the uniqueness of God's work as a Creator. Every human is a unique work of an omniscient God who surely labors over each one of us until He gets us special. But during no period in life is the human uniqueness more evident than during the junior high years. It seems, particularly to the outsider looking in, that all the juices of life—the emotions, the moods, the hungers, and passions—come to the surface for the very first time, and they come with such force that they shock and amaze the participants.

Let's face it. Junior high is a rough time. If you think it's rough for you as a parent, think for a moment about what the poor teenager is going through. Try to strut a few steps in his Nikes and boat shoes.

And that leads me to the purpose of this book. I have already told you that it is not a typical how-to book. There are simply too many extremes to be gathered up and grasped by a few generalities. Instead, I want to give you a glimpse of some "typical" junior high people involved in the very act of living, of doing and feeling, of acting and reacting.

These descriptive anecdotes are gathered from several years and several sources. I taught and coached junior high students for a lot of years, and I still visit junior high schools regularly. Many of my closest friends are presently dedicated, knowledgeable junior high teachers. And, if I may boast, I just promoted the youngest of my own three children to the beautiful age of fifteen and the "high schooler" title that goes with it. As a parent, I am now an expert. In other words, I have a perspective with distance.

As you will see, many of these episodes do originate in school, and you will probably wonder why. After all, I am supposed to be writing a book for parents. But my purpose is to help you understand—to help you get a glimpse of your junior higher in both natural and artificial settings; and the school is a dominant force in the overall lives of these people.

If your child shows certain attitudes and behavior at school, he will probably carry those home with him—and to church and to scouts and to every area of his life. By viewing our children in a school setting, we are able to gain a clearer perspective.

Your first thought as you read some of these vignettes may be, *My junior higher isn't like that at all.* But keep reading. I assure you that these stories are all close enough to reality to be disturbing. I may get to your child before I am finished. And who knows? He may evolve into one of the other characters before God is finished with him.

Perhaps a good question at this point would be, "Why do I need to write such a book and why do you need to read it?" Let me answer with an illustration.

The other evening, I attended one of those after-church parties of about five couples. The conversation turned to good times—especially stories about growing up—childhood and adolescence. It was a mixed group (regionally, I mean) with Southerners, Midwesterners, Easterners, and Canadians well represented.

Since we were all getting rather candid and loud and bold as we laughed at our youthful foibles, I decided to take advantage of the opportunity and do some research for this project.

So I said, "I'll tell you what let's do. Let's all remember one fun story about when we were in junior high."

Immediately, stillness gripped the room. Sheets of it blanketed the group. Laughter turned to silence. Dancing eyes stopped in their joy. Meditation marked the brows.

Well, there are two things teachers can't stand—we can't stand noise and we can't stand silence. So I decided I would make the exam a little easier. "Let's just remember one thing that happened to us, good or bad, when we were in junior high."

That got the same response. Silently, people started getting up and leaving. I think the hostess is still upset with me for breaking up the party.

But after having done that extensive research, a survey of

ten people, I have concluded that most of us adults have chosen not to remember our junior high years. We have simply stuffed those years way down deep in the memory box, hoping they never torment us again. But now, through the divinely ordained office of parenthood, we find ourselves having to help our own children struggle through the period that we are trying to forget. Perhaps when they need us the most, we are the least prepared to identify with what is happening to them.

That is why I have chosen this format for the book. Through these descriptions, perhaps I can remind you. If not, at least I can introduce you to some of the people and circumstances your junior higher encounters daily, and you should be in a little better position to function as a parent and at the same time keep your own sanity.

But I don't want to cast a negative note at the start. As I said before, junior high is a crucial time. The changes that occur during these three years are significant and consequential. And changes always come complete with apprehension and some turmoil.

But every adult I know has survived this age. And every set of parents I know who have adult children survived the times when "junior highs invaded their homes." Not only can you make it, but it could be a rather pleasant and educational experience.

Now, let's get back to Sherri.

2
Pledges, Promises, and Perceptions

"Why do her moods change so quickly?"

I present Sherri's story first in this series because it is one of the most typical. Maybe your junior higher has already demonstrated something like this to you. If not, he or she may at least feel like it.

Since the incident is rather typical, it should provide us with some valuable insights into life from Sherri's point of view so we can at least understand, even during the times when we feel inadequate to help.

Why did Sherri react so violently and heal so quickly? Why did this normally sweet, cooperative, popular young lady forsake all her dignity and poise to make a point with a temper tantrum that she didn't even approve of herself?

I am not sure I have all the answers, and I don't want to oversimplify the complex causes of any behavior. But I will offer some ideas that might help us understand Sherri, and any other Sherri who might be living at your house.

Assuming that temper tantrums are not normal behavior for Sherri (it was the first one I or my colleagues at school had seen), and assuming that Sherri was not intentionally experimenting with a new method of manipulating adults (we will get to this later), there had to be some cause for her behavior, which actually shocked both of us. My guess is that it was disappointment.

At this point in her development, Sherri's life is characterized by change and flux. There are very few things that are stable and dependable. Her friends change. One day they are short and cutesy fat; the next day they are tall and lean. One day they sing tenor; the next day they sing bass.

And Sherri herself is changing. Think about life from her vantage point for a moment. When you are that age, looking into the mirror is like looking at the mountains. Every day you see something you have never seen before. Even though you may like what you see, you are still a little worried about how it will all work out in the end. One day you are beautiful; the next day you have a pimple on your nose. There is always some risk.

With these changes in appearance come changes in personalities. Friendly people become sour; sour people become popular. Straight friends start stealing nips from their daddy's liquor cabinet, and they prod you to join them. You tell your best friend your latest secret crush, and the next day you catch her flirting with him. Promises are broken; dependable people can't be trusted, and you are constantly bracing yourself to expect the unexpected.

Such is the undercurrent of life for Sherri. She may not be conscious of all this; but it is there and she can feel it even if she doesn't know it.

Surely, Sherri is entitled to something dependable and constant and consistent. What shall she choose? Teacher! It has a ring of promise to it. Most teachers she has met have been fairly nice. Since they are around kids, they should understand her needs. And besides, the position itself means authority and respect. All her life she has been taught that; so now, when she needs dependability she throws her trust onto the title of teacher, and onto me, specifically.

When I didn't show for our appointment, I not only forsook her trust, but I undermined her source of consistency. I became just another undependable nuisance she would have to tolerate. She didn't want that from me. She wanted authority and consistency. When I didn't deliver, she tried to get back at my inconsistency by doing something inconsistent herself. It was more than an attack on me. It was a statement of her disappointment.

If ours had been a daughter–parent relationship, and I had committed such a breach of her expectation, Sherri would still have had to react. She might have run away from home. That seems to be a rather common way for a junior higher to handle such a setback. It is actually more common than I ever thought

In recent years, I have asked hundreds of well-adjusted college students if they ever ran away from home. About 30 percent sheepishly hang their heads, study their shoe shine with feigned intensity, clear their throats several times, then quietly relate their experience when, in total frustration, they summoned up as much courage as they could find, packed a small bag, and left home forever. Of course, most were back in a matter of hours, and the event now lies only in their memories as a source of embarrassment, especially when asked to expose themselves to amateur psychologists.

The explanation for this now regrettable behavior is almost always the same—the dependability of the adult world broke down. These people had to lash out against the perceived injustice, and this was the most serious form of rebellion they could think of.

Of course, these protests come in many forms and degrees, depending on the established relationships with the adult authority, the perceived seriousness of the injustice, and the personality of the junior higher. Some may, as my college students admit, run away from home for a couple of hours. Some may run away from home for a few months. Some may lock themselves in their rooms for a few hours and sob themselves to sleep. Some may simply slam the door when they leave. Some may only fester inside until the incident is forgotten or replaced with a more positive experience. But regardless of how it shows itself, the hurt is probably there every time the junior higher's limited source of stability is shaken.

Now, let's see if we can translate this whole event into some suggestions for parents.

A. Be Consistent

In simple and obvious language, be consistent. "Okay," you say, "I have heard that so many times it is just another cliché. Tell me something new and pertinent." But I'm serious. If your child is now approaching this age of early adolescence, it is time for you to take a hard look at the operational meaning of consistency in parenting. I realize that if you are the kind of parent concerned enough to read books to help you in your task, you have already made a great effort to be consistent, and your child and I thank you. But now the challenge is even greater. Not only is your consistency very critical to your child, but it gets harder to be consistent. As life gets more complex, the arbitrary lines of decisions grow grayer. It is not going to be as easy as it has been to say yes and no.

For one thing, when your child was younger, consistency was a matter of remembering what you said and keeping your word. But as your child grows into a new level of awareness and perception and begins to read into the subtleties of behavior and intentions, you have to back that word up with something. Consistency now means living what you say.

Let me put this into a definite suggestion. Now that you are facing a greater demand for a more complex level of consistency, I am going to encourage you and your spouse to spend some time together making sure that the home front is unified. You could take a weekend off, go somewhere together, and talk until you have reached an agreement about how the two of you are going to react to some of the issues your junior higher is going to thrust upon you during the next few years. Let me suggest some topics worthy of such attention.

1. Dating—How early and how intense? Which of you is going to explain the facts of life and when? How deep are you going to go into that explanation? What will you do if you don't approve of your child's selection?

2. Curfew—Not only do you need to agree on the hours, but you need to agree on the consequences when the curfew is broken. "Breathes there a teenager with soul so dead who never to himself has said, *Aw shucks, I can be late because my parents are already in bed.*"

3. Friends—Whom do you like? Are you going to interfere in the friend selection (subtlely, of course) by emphasizing church activities? How are you going to handle a bad friend choice?

4. Grades—What are your expectations? Are they realistic? How are you going to react if your expectations are not met?

5. Activities—Are you going to insist on certain participation? How are you going to support your child's participation when he is involved?

6. Dress and appearance—What kinds of standards are you going to set, and who has the responsibility to enforce them?

7. *Drugs and alcohol*—Who is responsible for the instruction? How are you going to react if you discover that your child is experimenting?

8. *Church activities*—How much are you going to insist on? Are you going to require Sunday night and mid-week attendance? Are you going to request (or demand) that the junior higher sit with the family during services?

9. *Temper tantrums* (or other forms of rebellion)—Do you punish, panic, or ignore?

10. *Parental roles*—Most children tend to talk to one parent about certain areas of their lives but talk to the other about other areas. Are you and your spouse aware of these roles and are you comfortable with them?

There you have it, but I offer this list of issues as a starting point. My purpose is to recommend that you and your spouse have discussed and reached some kind of agreement on some of the basic but crucial problems which will occur during the junior high years. The list could, of course, be much longer; but if you have at least agreed on a few things, you will probably find yourself compatible on other issues as they happen. The important thing is that your junior higher's parents provide him with a model of consistency and stability.

B. Make No Promises You Can't Keep

This is probably just a repetition of the first point, but I am not afraid of being repetitive. The point is worth learning. I am sure you are not the kind of parent who intentionally lies to your child; but during the junior high years, it is important that you carry out all promises. If you promise a hockey game on Thursday, you really should take him to the hockey game on Thursday. If you promise grounding if he breaks curfew, you really should ground him if he breaks curfew.

C. Analyze Your Own Life for Stressful Changes

In recent years we have read some strong warnings about stress-producing changes in an adult's life. We have learned to be cautious about our own mental and physical health during such times as retirement, divorce, surrendering the last child to adulthood, unemployment, moving, or changing jobs. But at the same time we should recognize that our children also undergo some stress during those times of change, particularly if it is during a period when the child's life is characterized by change.

If you are in the age bracket to have a junior-high-age child, you may very well be looking at some significant changes in your own life. This may be the time when you are thinking about moving out of your starter home to something more permanent. You may be considering a promotion that would drastically (or even slightly) alter your life-style. Your relationship with your spouse may be growing in one direction or another.

Of course, you can't avoid these changes. You wouldn't want to; but I do suggest that you realize that these stress-producing situations also cause some stress in your children, particularly when they are at that stage when their whole world is changing.

D. Don't Close Doors Behind Your Junior Higher

When I didn't show for my appointment with Sherri, she reacted with a rather unusual type of behavior. She was angry at the time, and her feeling for me was definitely one of hatred. That may sound a bit strong, but I really think she hated me at the time. It was an honest emotion that came with the moment, and she had to try it on to see how it fit. By the next morning, she had realized that hatred wasn't appropriate. At least, it wasn't the way she wanted to feel about me; so then she was faced with a new challenge. She had to glue her courage to the sticking place and try to come back into the relationship at a place where we had been before the hurricane hit. That took some real integrity and character on her part.

I suppose we could make a case for my demanding some act of penance from her. I had been wronged, at least partially. I could have threatened or at least demanded an apology. But I am not sure that was necessary. She had discovered on her own that the emotion was wrong. Through the incident, she had grown. What was important now was for me to accept her cheerfulness and her willingness to forget as apology enough.

Although it was probably by accident, I think I handled the situation right. I hadn't closed any doors behind her. She knew that when she was ready she could come home and be welcomed.

This idea isn't original with me. I found it in Luke 15. When the prodigal son decided to come home after squandering all his inheritance, the father not only made it easy for him, but even threw a party.

So through Sherri's progression from outburst to congeniality, we see a junior higher's plea for stability and dependability amidst her world of change and experimentation and adjustment, and we see our own responsibility for providing as much consistency for her as possible. Or, on the other hand, it might have been that she just felt like a little demonstration at the time. Oh well, let's look at some other people to see whether there are other lessons to be learned.

We can begin with a study of body changes.

3
Vernon and Roger: The Long and Short of It

"How big will they be when they get to junior high?"

Vernon and Roger were on the seventh-grade basketball team together. Roger was one of the most responsible thirteen-year-olds I have ever known. He was always the first one to practice, but that is understandable because he kept his locker neat and orderly. He didn't have to hunt for his shoes or report one of his socks stolen.

He was neat. He took care of his equipment. And he was always the first one out to practice. Once on the practice floor, Roger did everything the coach asked. When the players ran laps, he always ran next to the wall and didn't cheat on the corners, even when the coach wasn't looking. When the coach blew his whistle, Roger stopped dribbling and ran in to hear what the coach said. Roger bought a stocking cap because Coach said to cover his head after practice. When Coach said to shoot with the left hand, Roger worked on it at home until he could do it. Not only did Roger know his own position, he also knew where every other player was supposed to be at all times. In short, Roger was a very responsible person and player.

On the other hand, one might have gotten the idea that Vernon didn't care. He was late to practice almost every day, and he even skipped some days. Actually, the teachers sometimes kept him after school so he had an excuse, but he still missed practice. His locker was in shambles. His socks never matched. When lap time came, Vernon loafed and cut corners. When Coach blew his whistle, Vernon always took time to shoot another basket before he came in. And he never listened when Coach talked. That was evident by the way he played. Vernon never knew where he was supposed to be, and he was always in the wrong place. The coach had to hold up practice just to tell Vernon where to go. In short, Vernon was a very irresponsible person and player.

But I forgot to mention that Roger was four six and Vernon was an even six feet tall and well-developed for his age.

As the day of the first game approached, Roger got excited. A couple of days before, the coach checked out uniforms. They might have looked like old eighth-grade hand-me-downs to you, but to Roger they were on par with what the Chicago Bulls wear. He didn't mind that he was the last one to get the uniform. That wasn't significant. What was important was that he had one. After his mother tucked it in for him a bit, he hung it on his door so he could look and dream.

On the day of the game, he was the first one into the dressing room, as always. He dressed quickly and waited for Coach to come give that powerful speech before they went out on the floor. When the coach got there, what he saw first was Vernon—leaning against the locker, still in street clothes. Vernon had forgotten his uniform. Coach ranted and raved and talked of responsibility, while Vernon hung his head and grinned. Finally, Coach devised a plan. Vernon would just have to wear Roger's uniform, even if it looked ridiculous on him, and Roger could sit on the bench and keep shot charts.

"Fiend," you shout. "Foul! What a horrible man. How could he do such a despicable thing?" But I ask you, while we are waiting for the tar to get hot, if you had been a young coach trying to win at the seventh-grade level so you could keep your job and someday move up to high school coaching, would you have let a six-foot giant sit on the bench on the small technicality that he had forgotten his uniform?

Aren't these the realities of life? Roger wasn't going to play in the game anyway! Wouldn't it have been more dishonest to let him put on the uniform just so he could shoot around during warm-ups? When do we teach people the hard, cruel facts of life? In fact, what *did* this young coach teach both these boys and the whole team that day? That winning is the only thing that matters? That responsibility doesn't count for much? That life always favors the naturally gifted? And are these lessons all that false?

But I digress. These are important questions which merit some serious consideration, but I just threw them in here to illustrate how many of us often unknowingly and unintentionally teach (indoctrinate) our own values to junior highers whose perceptions may be keener than we think. I would like this incident to lie in the backs of our minds and haunt us a bit every time we make a quick decision or take an action affecting a learning, growing, changing, adapting young person.

But let's get back to analyzing the coach's action. Whether we agree with him or not, we need to look at some of the basic factors at work here, and see what we can learn from them.

1. Size—This is obvious. There was a foot and a half difference between these two guys. That may be a little extreme; but such differences are common at this age. Not only are there differences between individuals, but any one person may encounter a serious size change in what seems like a matter of days.

Vernon himself probably grew six inches over the summer, and Roger may grow six inches the next summer. Pity the poor mothers who are trying to keep these guys in clothes, particularly if they are the kind of kids who are worried about how they look. Fortunately, that attitude hadn't come to Vernon yet, so he wouldn't have minded if his pants were four inches short.

Just to give this discussion some practical value, I offer some suggestions on how to keep these growing people in style without destroying the whole family clothes budget. (I concentrate on sons here. The daughters add another burden.)

- Sew elastic in their cuffs and persuade them that knickers are in this year.
- Start a fad of leg warmers for men.
- Buy pads and have them walk on their knees.
- Buy long-tailed shirts so they can just keep pulling their pants down as the legs grow.
- Sew ruffles on the bottoms of their pants!

As you can see, I don't have any solutions, so let me mention a couple of other obvious problems associated with this size difference. Can you imagine how much more food it takes to fill that foot-and-a-half vacuum? And just another question for your consideration: If you had a thirteen-year-old son the size of Roger, would you feel as guilty about asking him to share a room with a smaller brother as you would if he were Vernon's size?

And this leads us to a more complex problem created by this size difference.

2. *Expectations*—Sure, we realize that these guys are both thirteen years old. We also realize that Roger is more dependable and, in many ways, more mature than Vernon. We realize this from the word descriptions. In fact, I played a bit of a trick on you by withholding the size information until you had formulated some opinion of both boys.

But let's put these two thirteen-year-olds side by side. Can you honestly say that you are capable of treating them as equals? If the two of them showed up to do some yard work for you, could you pay them the same salary without any misgivings?

And this is one of the most serious challenges for people who work with junior highers—learning to accept the fact that a person does not mature in all aspects of his character on the same schedule and learning to realize that physical maturity is often deceptive. Roger was the more mature, but he would have a hard time convincing his coach and most adults of that. Of course, Vernon had feelings. The coach could see that. Anyone that big is permitted and expected to have strong feelings about equity and justice. But what could Roger know? If he had any maturity at all, he wouldn't be so little. The coach's decision wouldn't affect Roger. He wasn't big enough to care.

There is actually injustice here on both sides. Roger's potential and maturity are often ignored. In most people's eyes, he is still a child and unless he develops physically, he will be treated as a child for the next two years. We give him the responsibility of a child and we expect him to act like a child. When he acts with more maturity, we say, "What a nice child!"

On the other hand, not only is Vernon saddled with all that size, but he is also burdened with people's greater expectations. They expect him to perform with more maturity than he actually has at this point. If Roger had forgotten his uniform, the coach would have probably ignored the incident. But Vernon, although he gets to play, will still have to run extra laps as punishment.

Age is no factor here. The bigger one is, the more is expected of him. And Vernon simply does not have the intellectual or emotional maturity to handle the adult responsibility demanded of him.

He, like Roger, has a natural need to punch, pester,

choke, squeak, slouch, stumble, belch, drop, and forget. He gets just as excited about a new hair on his chest and just as upset about a new pimple on his nose. Even if he *has* just scored twenty-five points in the basketball game, he still may trip over a line and fall on his face on his way to the dressing room. And it is then that we need to remember that he is just another thirteen-year-old boy.

This is one of the most difficult problems of the whole junior high scene. It is difficult for Vernon and Roger, and it is difficult for the people who have to work with them. If you are going to be effective as a parent, you have to develop some method of going beyond size and physical development to assess maturity. You will just have to keep telling yourself that thirteen-year-olds are thirteen years old regardless of how often they shave.

The coach couldn't see that. I pray that you can.

Now, let's see how that problem affects girls.

4
When Beauty Comes Early

"She looks so grown-up. I'm really glad she is going to miss all the problems of that awkward age."

I remember the first time I ever saw Helen. I was eating lunch in the school cafeteria, sharing the hour with some of my colleagues, an average collection of junior high teachers discussing such high-level issues as nuclear disarmament and why the Cowboys never win the Super Bowl. Suddenly, right in the midst of all this profoundness, the conversation stopped. I looked up from my food to see what had shocked us into a state of silence, an unusual condition for a junior high lunchroom, even at the teacher's table, and I saw Helen standing in line.

Simply stated, she was strikingly beautiful—a real conversation stopper. As I began to fumble in my mind with who she might be—an especially mature high school student visiting our building, a student teacher from a nearby college, a young mother—the principal, probably anticipating our questions, said, "That's Helen, the new seventh grader who transferred in this morning."

We sat shocked. As junior high teachers, we had come to expect size and maturity differences in young people; but Helen was the most extreme example we had ever seen.

As we became acquainted with her in class, we discovered that she had the personality, intelligence, and talent to match her beauty. She was just a graceful person. Although she was not that much sharper than the average seventh grader, she had a certain confidence about herself that carried over into her academic work. She also was cheerful and cooperative.

At least, that is the impression that I have of Helen during those first months she was in our school. You have to realize that even my memories might be a bit out of line. Because she was so mature physically, that was the kind of person the other teachers and I expected her to be. If she had not had an assignment on time, we would have been more likely to accept her excuse than if she had looked like any other seventh grader. I don't tell an adult, "Eat your liver before you can have dessert," and I don't think I would have told Helen that either.

As the new kid on the block, Helen was not as enthusiastically accepted by her classmates as she was by the teachers. To understand this, one needs to know something about the junior high caste system. Since I will discuss this in detail in a later chapter, let me oversimplify it here by saying that there are two dominant groups in a junior high school—the in group and the out group. The in group is composed of athletes, cheerleaders, and all the other students who have learned how to get their ego rewards from the system. They are the students who have experienced success and satisfaction working within the established structure. Since they have been rewarded by the system, they are generally cooperative and congenial.

On the other hand, the out group members have not achieved enough distinction and success within the established order to give them any great definition of self-worth. So by the time they get into seventh grade, most of them have chosen to seek their identification outside the system itself.

In most cases, the in group is fairly well established. Since these people know they belong and know they are the really important people in school, they really do not have to open their membership rolls. Any time the in group reaches out and accepts a new student, it is actually an act of charity, of condescension. (Getting accepted is usually a bit easier for a guy, particularly if he is an athlete.)

But that group couldn't condescend to accept Helen. She was too mature and too pretty. She would have to have come into the group as the leader, and the present leadership didn't want that. So she stayed outside the in group.

On the other hand, the out group is usually easier to get into. Since these people are a little lonely anyway, they welcome new members. So they adopted Helen. But she didn't fit in there either. At this point, she wasn't angry with the system. She was still worried about her studies and grades, and pleasing teachers and parents.

Although she was gracious and bright enough not to offend anybody, she was never really comfortable with the people who were willing to accept her. Consequently, she spent her year in seventh grade being more popular with adults than with the people her own age. That was fine with the adults. We all enjoyed her friendship.

However, near the end of the year, Helen revealed her true value system. She made an emphatic statement about what she wanted in life. She wanted to be a typical, popular junior high girl. In other words, she wanted to be a cheerleader. She wanted to wave the pompoms, chew bubble gum, and yell for the football team.

So when tryouts came, she was one of the first to sign up. At our school, cheerleader tryouts were one of the major rites of the year. As one of their last contributions to the alma mater, the outgoing eighth graders engineered the festivities, and each group tried with ever increasing optimism to outdo everything that had ever been done before.

On the appointed day, the student body marched into the gym to the accompaniment of the band's playing the "Washington Post March." With giggling sincerity, the outgoing captain made her farewell speech, a rousing plea for school spirit. Then, participating in pairs, the aspirants led the student body in a cheer as they demonstrated their talents at hollering and waving at the same time. Although Helen looked a bit out of place because she was about a foot taller than her partner, she was, nevertheless, graceful through the whole ordeal.

But when the students cast their secret ballots at the end of the ritual, Helen wasn't even close. She wasn't even close enough to be an alternate.

During the summer, I heard that Helen was modeling for one of the local stores. When school started the next fall, she was going steady with a high school junior who owned a nice car and a questionable reputation. After that, she only went through the motions of being in junior high. By the time she was seventeen, she had become actively involved in the drug culture, had dropped out of school, and had moved in with a man several years older than she. I am not sure where she is or what she is doing now.

I realize that Helen is a bit of an unusual case. She was not only mature, but also beautiful at thirteen; but she still represents a troublesome group—the junior high girls who mature physically before they do emotionally and intellectually. Helen made a strong effort to fit into her own age group, but at that point in a person's development, the age group is rather narrowly defined. In high schools, sophomores are frequently comfortable with seniors. In adulthood, there isn't that much difference between the thirties and the fifties. But in the stage of early adolescence, seventh graders are seventh graders and eighth graders are eighth graders.

When Helen couldn't find her niche among her own age group, she had to look outside. In other words, she had to experiment. She knew she wasn't an adult, so she settled for the next step up, the high schoolers. Maybe she could find some companionship there.

But once she paid her dues into that group, she was suddenly thrust into decisions she wasn't prepared to make. Helen was not experienced enough nor mature enough emotionally to make rational decisions about how to handle such things as drugs or her own sexuality; but because of the way she looked, these decisions were forced on her at a time when peer acceptance was about her only base for value judgments. That is a difficult thing for anybody—to try to live your life on the basis of what you think other people want you to do. Small wonder that she became confused, disenchanted, and eventually hardened.

Helen also teaches us another important lesson. There is a vast difference between thirteen-year-olds and sixteen-year-olds. Sometimes those differences may not be immediately obvious. Thirteen-year-olds may look older, and they may even sound older. Many seventh graders can read and write and talk as intelligently as many high school juniors. But those three to five years of studying at the University of Life have their impact.

Now that we have examined this sad case, we probably ought to spend some time asking ourselves what could have been done to prevent Helen's unhappiness and her subsequent disillusionment. The answer to that, though, is more difficult than I would like it to be. It is not too easy for parents or teachers to manipulate a group of seventh and eighth graders into accepting someone. We could have told Helen that being a cheerleader was not all that important, but I don't think she would have believed us. We could have been closer to her ourselves, but she didn't want adult friendship. She already had that. What she really wanted was to be a seventh grader among seventh graders.

Helen's parents were intelligent, caring people who had successfully brought her older brothers and sisters through junior high age without any permanent scars. What went wrong this time? The answer is simple but painful. Helen was a normal, sweet, young girl who had the body of a woman. The people she encountered were more aware and more interested in the woman than in the girl; thus, we—teachers, classmates, and parents—unknowingly cheated her out of three critical years of development.

If you have a daughter who is maturing physically more rapidly than in other areas, I offer Helen's story just as it stands. Obviously, I am suggesting understanding, concern, and sensitivity. Your daughter may look like she is past this stage, but she is still a junior higher with all the trappings thereof. Make sure you don't forget that.

5
When Beauty Fades Early

"No wonder she's not popular anymore. She's so sullen and cross. She used to be so sweet. What happened to her when she started junior high?"

The teacher was trying to teach the seventh graders the concept of romanticism—the idea that something in the distance looks good but in reality isn't as much fun as you thought it was going to be. The concept was important to their understanding a short story about Southerners preparing for the Civil War.

To make the experience as personal as possible, the teacher asked, "Have any of you really looked forward to some event, and then when it came, you were totally disappointed by how it turned out?"

Patsy's answer was terse and spontaneous. "Yeah. Junior high."

Patsy wasn't just having a bad day. Her appraisal was accurate and permanent. So far, her seven months in junior high had been totally disappointing, and things weren't getting any better.

Patsy had a special kind of problem. She had been in school with many of her classmates since they started in kindergarten. Very early, she had become everybody's favorite—students and teachers alike. She was both pretty and cheerful. She had a nice smile and a heart big enough to share it with people, so her classmates loved and envied her at the same time.

She was a good student and she had a quick wit, so with

her combination of cute and neat, she was also the teacher's pet. But her classmates didn't resent her for that because she was so friendly. Later, as the students edged to the upper end of childhood and began to notice for the first time that the world was coeducational in structure, Patsy mastered the art of flirting. And she spread her smiles over a wide enough area to accumulate several male interests. But at the same time, she remained popular with the girls. In short, throughout elementary school, Patsy was the center of attention.

But during the summer between sixth and seventh grades, when people are supposed to mature and change, a strange thing happened. Instead of growing tall and feminine as her friends did, Patsy only put a few pounds on her already short stature; and on top of that, she put on the pounds in places not necessarily conducive to feminine charm.

When the students reconvened at the junior high in the fall to "ooh" and "ahh" at how much everybody had changed over the summer, Patsy soon lost her center-ring attraction. And to make matters worse, she was replaced by her best friend. Junior highers are fickle that way. Although no one intended to be rude to Patsy, it was just that the other girl looked like more fun, and people that age usually trust their eyes.

Patsy had enough class not to make any scenes, but she quietly went about trying to reclaim some of the distinction she had lost with the body changes. She became the first girl in class to wear eye makeup, and after intense pleading with her parents for two weeks, she got her ears pierced. Yet, despite all her attempts, those cosmetic improvements didn't really change things that much. Her best friend was still the center of attention, both with the boys and the girls, and Patsy was cast into a supporting role.

That change in roles never comes easily, particularly when a person has enjoyed stardom as long as Patsy had. And to make matters worse, that change in roles was dictated by something as superficial as change in body style. Going into junior high, Patsy inside was the same sweet, lovable person she had always been. The only thing that had changed was that she didn't look as good as her friend. Why should she be penalized for that?

Patsy's struggle however, was real and deep and fairly typical. As junior highers go through the body changes, they also encounter changes in their social roles. In this case, the popular person moved to the outskirts of the group. Of course, it was tough on her; but that change was also tough on her friend who was not ready for all the attention she was going to get because of the accidents of growth.

Patsy was a strong enough person to live through her junior high misery. She cried a lot; she was frequently sullen and moody; she spent a lot of time locked up in her room, and she bounced between hatred and loyalty for her classmates.

But she survived. In fact, during her junior year in high school, she managed to reclaim some of the popularity she had lost, and she finished her high school career on a rather positive note. Now that she is an adult, she has chosen to forget about junior high altogether, to block out of her mind all those unhappy memories of that period of transition.

If Patsy had been less of a person, that change in roles could have been devastating. In fact, I chose Patsy to illustrate this point because her story *does* end happily. I am sure she caused her parents some frustration. None of us is happy when our children are unhappy, and any good parent will search for some remedy that will work. Unfortunately, in Patsy's case, her parents were almost powerless to help. This was something that she had to go through alone.

If your child is nearing that age when body styles and appearance change rapidly, you may as well prepare yourself to suffer with him through some changes in social roles that come with the package. Although you can't really speed up the operation or change the course of it, you can provide some understanding and perhaps some diversion.

Perhaps the best help a parent can offer in this situation is to help the junior higher see past the present. Of course, this is tough for any of us, but if life is really miserable for everybody, it might be worth a try. Spend some time with your child reflecting about what life is going to be. Talk of adult things such as work, marriage, and family. Give him some adultlike responsibility.

If you promise not to tell, I'll share my secret weapon, which I save for my children when they are struggling through these critical periods of re-identification. I find a vacant parking lot somewhere, and I teach them how to drive. You would be amazed at how much thirty minutes at the wheel in an isolated parking lot can do for a thirteen-year-old's morale. I haven't resolved the problem. He isn't any more socially accepted, although he may brag about his driving skills all over school. But I have given him a glimpse of what life is going to be like once he gets through this time, and that seems to help. Or at least I have helped him romanticize the next plateau of development.

6
Testing the Fences

*"He rebels at everything we say. Is he
really old enough to live without our rules?"*

When I glanced in the door, the classroom was in chaos.
The young teacher was doing his best to conduct a discussion on some fine point of American history, but the eighth
graders were hearing little of it.

Some girls in the back were busy with hair tools and
makeup chests preparing themselves for an afternoon encounter with some high school sophomores who came to our
building for basketball practice. Some of the boys, bothered
by the girls' insensitivity to their needs for female attention,
had swiped one of the purses and were playing a rather
competent game of keep-away. Three or four other boys
were busy with one of those new beeping computer games.
The more attentive students interrupted their own personal
discussions on occasions to answer one of the teacher's
questions with a smart reply designed to bring tons of hilarity to all within hearing distance.

As principal, I could have gone in and stopped the mess
and restored order. The students would have respected my
office enough to respond to my presence. For one thing, they
knew I had the ability to "get them into trouble." But I decided against going in. My presence would only serve to undermine what little authority the young teacher still had.
There had to be a better way to help him and the class
through this adjustment period.

I wandered on down to my office expecting a visitor. In

about ten minutes, Scott walked through my door. That in itself interested me. That whole classroom was in an uproar. How in the world could that young teacher single out one individual who was solely responsible for the general chaos? Of course, I knew what the teacher was doing. He had to take some measure. He could not ignore the inconsideration, so he picked out the most vocal person to serve as an example. This may not be the right way to handle the problem, but teachers and parents resort to it frequently. We sometimes do use people as examples.

"Scott," I asked, "are you in trouble again?" Scott had been in my office before.

"Yeah, but it's not my fault."

"What's not your fault?"

"It's not my fault that I'm in trouble."

"Why isn't it your fault? You *are* the one in my office."

"It's not my fault because he's a lousy teacher."

"What do you mean, he is a lousy teacher?"

"He can't control the classroom."

"But, Scott, I just came from your classroom, and you are the worst one in there."

"That's what I said. He can't control me. He's a lousy teacher, and I shouldn't get in trouble just because he can't control the class."

Now figure that one out. What was Scott trying to tell teachers and parents about himself and many of his friends with that piece of logic? What lesson can we learn?

Actually, it seems obvious enough. Scott and the rest of the class were simply trying to find the fences. They were looking for the boundaries. They didn't really like that chaotic situation any more than the teacher did, but they were depending on him to establish the guidelines. When he, through his inexperience, failed to do so, the class had to keep flailing until someone imposed some limits. For these eighth graders, this was another form of experimentation.

Notice first of all that Scott did not have the personal discipline to build his own fences. He needed some kind of external authority curtailing his behavior; when he couldn't find it, he was frustrated and angry. Although he kept experimenting, he would have felt better about the situation if he had bumped into the boundaries before his behavior actually got out of hand. He wasn't pleased with himself, but he knew he wasn't to be blamed. It was the teacher's fault.

Although Scott would have probably complained about the boundaries when he first found them, he would have abided by them once he knew they were fixed. And he would have probably been happier for it because, in a strange, paradoxical way, he would have had more freedom. Try that one on for size. The more rigid the boundaries, the more freedom Scott would have had within the boundaries. That is not an absolute or universal principle, but it is applicable to a majority of junior highers. Most of them are simply trying to discover how strong the fences are.

And this is a point that may confuse young teachers and parents. In order to find out where those fences are, the junior higher has to experiment; he has to test; he has to war against the boundaries themselves to make sure they are real and not just inconvenient facades. In other words, the junior higher's normal reaction is to complain about the rules and restrictions; and if you listen to him, you may get the idea that he really resents their being there. You might get the idea that all those restrictions are limiting him and may give him all kinds of neuroses. And that might be true for some. But more often, all that complaining and testing is just the junior higher's way of finding out where the real boundaries are. Once he gets that settled, he will probably be perfectly content to live within the boundaries or accept the consequences for violating them.

It is appropriate for your thirteen-year-old child to say,

sometimes even in loud and animated tones, "I don't *want* to go to Grandma's house for Thanksgiving. I am *not* going to Grandma's house for Thanksgiving. You can't *make* me go to Grandma's house for Thanksgiving. There is *absolutely* nothing for me to do there. I'm going to stay home and go over to Bill's and play touch football and run around all day. But I am *not* going to Grandma's house!" Let me repeat: It is perfectly appropriate for him to say that, and if you have heard it, don't despair. It isn't meant to be a personal attack on you or Grandma. It is simply his way of saying, "Are you serious? Do you really want me to go to Grandma's house for Thanksgiving?"

How you respond to this bit of testing the fences depends on your personality. I, since it is appropriate with my style, would resort to firm levity: "Ha-ha. You're such a funny person. To think that I could spend a Thanksgiving at Grandma's without you. You're so funny we have to have you in the car for entertainment, or none of us could make the trip. Yep, as I think about it, I do believe you *will* go to Grandma's house for Thanksgiving."

Now, I know the risk I am running here. He will go, but he may not be all that much fun to be around. Nevertheless, we have at least established the boundaries. Since I have settled one question for him, I have now provided him with the freedom to experiment in other areas. Despite all his complaining, he prefers this to chaos.

I will conclude this incident with Scott with a summary and a warning.

1. *Don't be afraid to set the boundaries.* You are the adult in the relationship. Your child is looking for some guidance from you. Give it to him.
2. *Don't be shocked by all the testing of the boundaries once they are in place.* How else will he know that you are really serious?

3. *Keep your word despite the testing.* Be firm. If he violates the boundaries, make sure he accepts the preestablished consequences.

And now for the warning.

Not all junior highers are just testing to see where the fences are. Some are actually squeezed in by the structure and are lodging a deeper form of protest. Many of the points in this chapter and in this book, for that matter, are generalized. They fit most junior highers. But I urge you to have a close enough relationship with your own child to know how he is unique, how he doesn't fit the mold.

The exciting challenge of being a parent of a junior higher is the demand for creativity. By watching the group we can make some general observations and plan some specific strategies, but since every day brings changes, we constantly have to rearrange and redirect. Just as the junior higher learns by experimentation—trial and error—so parents can learn too. And we get to learn all over again with each child, because no two are alike. Isn't parenting exciting as well as educational!

The following section of chapters focusing on junior high social adjustments continues this theme of similarities and diversity.

7
Castes and Outcasts

*"There are so many people at that school.
How will he ever make friends and how
will he find his place in the crowd?"*

One of the best ways to learn about any wild beast is to study the pack with which it associates. This is particularly true with junior highers because the grouping is very important to most of them. Most junior highers spend a good part of their mental energy and their time trying to achieve and maintain some kind of status within a specific social group. Their efforts reveal that it is important to them to belong; so any study of how any one junior higher behaves and responds will require some analysis of that group which is setting the standards for his thinking, behavior, and appearance. If you want to understand your own junior higher, you need to understand something about the kind of group he is in and the kind of group he wants to be in.

With some caution about oversimplification and the dangers of generalization, we can classify most junior highers into four groups: the Jocks, the Brains, the Regulars, and the Burnouts.

Jocks

Although in its literal sense the term *Jocks* refers specifically to athletes, it has a broader definition in actual operation. The group usually identified by this term consists not only of the athletes and cheerleaders, it also includes the students who actively support school activities. (These also may be called Socialites.)

These people are everywhere and into everything. They play sports, lead cheers, print the newspaper, play in the band, get parts in the play, make friends with the teachers, and win all the awards at the annual assembly. But they are also active outside the school. They are officers in the church youth group; they volunteer for local ministries; and they are the leaders in scouts and other community groups.

In other words, these people are trying to find happiness in being productive, active, and cooperative—by working within the system rather than fighting against it. Although most of them encounter some frustrations and setbacks which naturally flow from all the changes they face, they still are basically satisfied with the general quality of life.

Usually, they tend to worry about how they look and what adults think about them; so they keep themselves clean according to junior high standards, and they try to make the best grades they can without earning the label of being scholarly.

In most schools, this is the old, established group. These people have been friends before, so it seems natural for them to stay together during junior high. Although these sweet, innocent children would never intentionally hurt anybody, the group tends to be closed to outsiders. Once this group is established, it is difficult for anyone to break in. Helen had this problem, but she is not alone. In fact, the exclusiveness of this Jock Club may present one of the cruelest structures of junior high life. How often I have stayed awake at night and prayed for that poor child who wants to be friends with a cheerleader who is already so popular that she doesn't have time for any more friends! It isn't as if that cheerleader wants to be cruel. She would even deny it. But her tight schedule and limited friendship circle become the cruelest form of rejection for those people who need her attention.

Although this problem exists for boys, it is probably not quite as rigid as it is for girls. For one thing, boys usually have more opportunities to achieve status than girls do. Any boy who participates in sports can usually make it into this club if he wants, and he might actually rise to a position of leadership just by his athletic activity.

Although there is a need for experimentation, chance, and risk among the Jocks, the members of this group are usually not as defiant as those of the other groups. They may operate on the fringe of structured rules and procedures, but they aren't really trying to destroy the system or live outside it. After all, the system has provided them with the rewards that help them identify themselves; so they want structure to prevail—even if they have to test it once in a while.

The Brains

I use the label *Brains* to classify a rather select group of junior highers who aren't ashamed to appear intellectual. Although the club isn't sexually exclusive, it tends to be male-dominated.

In many ways the members of this group look and act like normal (if there is such a thing) junior highers. They have growth spurts, voice changes, and skin problems. Like most of their contemporaries they fluctuate in behavior, attitudes, and interests somewhere between childhood and middle age.

But the Brains differ from the Jocks because they don't have enough time to be involved in all those childish activities such as basketball and cheering. They are simply too busy with chess or poetry or computers or science fiction or intricate science fair projects or whatever is in the intellectual spotlight at the moment they happen to find themselves caught in junior high.

Since this group is smaller than the Jocks, its members

tend to build close friendships with each other. If they are unhappy with not being in the popular group, they rarely mention it. On the other hand, members of this crowd may establish some friendships with adults with similar interests.

Perhaps the unusual characteristic about the Brains is that they may not make the best grades. Many leave grade success to the Jocks who need the attention, and they settle for applying themelves to their private interests.

I once met a junior high girl who had just published a book of poetry. Although it wasn't quite *Letters from the Portuguese,* it was still worth reading on a rainy Saturday. When I stopped by her class to congratulate her, I had to wait my turn. The teacher was reminding the young author that she was going to earn a D in English for the semester.

The Regulars

In the junior high caste system, the Regulars are the equivalent of what politicians once called the silent majority. These are the people who go through life, at least the junior high part of it, without attracting much attention.

This is not to say that they don't have their problems. They have as many growth and adjustment problems as the most active and popular Jock; but since they themselves aren't really big deals to anyone, their problems don't seem like big deals either.

It isn't so much that anyone dislikes them. It is just that no one seems to pay a lot of attention to them. Although they don't distinguish themselves with any great achievements like the Jocks, they don't cause too much trouble either.

Although most of them don't seem to be too dissatisfied with their lot in life, for some reason, perhaps apparent and perhaps not, these people simply have not made it into the big-time world of being a Jock. They just lack the aggressiveness or the confidence necessary to make themselves distinctive in the minds of the people who have the ability to make them important.

For example, in a typical class situation, the teacher may give as much as 80 percent of his positive reinforcement to the five Jocks, as much as 80 percent of his negative reinforcement to the five Burnouts, and forget the twenty Regulars altogether.

As I mentioned earlier, one of the saddest scenes in junior high social life is to see a Regular trying to break into the Jock Club. The Jocks aren't cruel, but they just don't have time for any more membership.

To parents and teachers, the Regulars present the biggest challenge. Although some of this casting system occurs in elementary school, it really comes to a head in junior high; so it is here that the Regular needs to learn how to deal with himself and his position in society.

The problem is that the standard used to classify him as a Regular is unrealistic and temporary. For whatever reasons he is left out of the in group, these reasons may change during this period of transition. And when these changes occur, the Regular needs to have enough confidence in himself to utilize his talents.

In other words, being a Regular can be a self-fulfilling prophecy. If a student learns in junior high that he isn't mature enough to participate in various activities, he may decide never to try again, even after he matures.

Let me emphasize this point. If your child gets cut from the seventh-grade basketball team and thus misses his right to be a Jock, encourage him to keep practicing and to keep trying for the next several years. He may grow; he may mature; and he may be the best high school basketball player in the class. But we won't know that if he lets his early setback destroy him.

At this age, grades become self-fulfilling prophecies. Too often students who make C's decide that they are "C people," and they go through life expecting C rewards and C opportunities. As parents who love these people for what they are at the moment they come to us, we can't let this kind of categorization internalize within these junior highers. We need to keep encouraging and recognizing the Regulars for what they can contribute.

I offer this as a warning, particularly if your junior higher happens to be a middle child or the second child of one sex. Since we as parents have been through this before, it is difficult to get excited about it the next time through; so we may, quite unintentionally, fail to give the second child as much attention, encouragement, or opportunity as the first one got. And the danger of this is that the Regular, if he gets dissatisfied with his nonconspicuous role, can either try to achieve some attention by moving into the Jock's world or look for the same results in the world of the Burnouts.

The Burnouts

These are the junior high people who have already had so many setbacks and frustrations that they have just decided not to cooperate with the established system anymore. Their protest ranges from overwhelming lethargy to open and hostile rebellion against all structure and authority.

It is difficult to pinpoint the exact reasons why a young person would make a decision not to try to get his attention and feelings of self-worth through the system. Perhaps he has a weakness in some learning skill such as reading, or perhaps he is not as good an athlete, or perhaps he is trying to follow the example of some older people, or perhaps he simply prefers this over the more energetic approach to life.

The unfortunate aspect of the junior high Burnout crowd is that many of them are destined to stay there. There are simply not as many options for fourteen-year-olds who have chosen not to participate in the established structure. Once they have made that decision, it is difficult for them to change their direction. For one thing, they get so far behind academically that it becomes almost impossible for them to catch up. Based on their junior high records, they will be directed into high school classes designed for them; and they will have fewer opportunities to interact with people outside their group.

This description of these people is a warning to all parents. Every person I know needs to succeed in any activity that takes much of his time. If he doesn't succeed, he loses interest, he quits trying, and he eventually seeks success or at least identification in an alternate activity. If your child meets only constant failure or frustration in class, or in activities, or in the church group, or even as your child, he will soon quit trying those activities and will begin to search for the alternatives. And somewhere there are some people who will accept him for what he is and will provide him the companionship and understanding he needs. Somewhere there are some people who will convince him that success isn't really that big a deal anyhow and that it is all right not to try. Actually, the group bonding may be stronger for Burnouts than for others. Since no one else accepts them, they accept each other.

In this chapter, I have used the school setting, but it is only a frame of reference. For the most part, junior highers stay in their groups. Jocks are Jocks wherever you meet them. Although a Regular may get a shot at leadership in another setting, such as church if there are no Jocks around, he is still a Regular for most of the time. In fact, most junior highers will in time internalize their roles in the casting system, and will begin to think of themselves in that role.

I do present this discussion with all sorts of warnings on the package. Labeling has to be the cruelest of human inventions, and is probably blasphemous. I don't think that at creation God said, "I think I will make a Jock this time."

Your child is a unique person who merits your special attention. But at the same time, he does function within the boundaries of a particular social group. If you want to provide your junior higher with some comforting and liberating understanding, you will need to understand something about the characteristics of the group he is in and the group he aspires to be in.

Knowing this may help you, for example, to understand the clothes he wears—the subject of the next chapter.

8
Purple Fingernails, Designer Socks, and Other Oddities

*"We have spent a small fortune on clothes
for him, yet he goes to school looking like a tramp."*

Now that we have defined one form of peer pressure, perhaps we should talk about one of the places where it is most obvious—junior high costuming. Actually, most junior highers seem to dress according to two standards, peer pressure and individuality.

Although these forces may rub against each other, they are not really as contradictory as they may sound. Peer pressure sets a standard of appearance that is broad enough to allow for individual decoration. Peer pressure may dictate that girls paint their nails, but the choice of color is theirs. Peer pressure may dictate that boys leave the top two buttons open, but the choice of the shirt is theirs. Or, for an illustration from my generation, peer pressure may dictate that the shirt be pink and the trousers charcoal; but the color of the belt, the crowning distinction, was my choice. (And I chose white—the one memory I have retained from my junior high days.)

Since we can't really fix the blame for the way junior highers look, the one thing for parents to understand is that for most of these people, appearance is very important. In fact, it may be as critical at the junior high age as at any period in one's life. Although you may not like the way your child looks, it may be almost necessary for him to look that way. Like the cowboy in the old West, every piece of the costume has a purpose—symbolic if not utilitarian.

The commitment to appearance seems to provide the junior higher with some sense of security in his constantly changing world, and it permits him a platform to make a statement to a world that isn't particularly interested in what he has to say.

And unless the situation gets completely out of hand, I am not convinced it is worth the effort and time to try to fight with a junior higher over the way he looks. I have known families who have drawn the battle lines sharply and have fought bitterly, frequently to no result except hard feelings and shaky relationships. But unless the person is indecent or irreverent or unclean, the issue probably doesn't justify the damage to the relationship.

Just before Larry's entry into eighth grade, we bought him several pairs of nice pants and some really pretty shirts. But in a few weeks, we noticed that he was wearing the same old jeans and shirt every day.

We encouraged, pleaded, begged, nagged, and finally ranted—all to no avail.

At Christmas we practiced deception. We quietly gave him a new pair of pants and a new shirt. *He can't reject a present,* we thought.

Since Larry is now a college student, free of any really conspicuous neuroses, we decided to give some of his old clothes away. We found that shirt and those pants tucked far into the back of his closet, still bearing the store tags. Five years later, the issue that provoked those arguments doesn't seem very important anymore.

One of the problems with junior high dress is a matter of double meaning. Some things have different meanings for adults than they do for the junior highers. One of the best places to realize this is in the language gap. I have known perfectly fine words that I have learned not to use with junior highers. I wouldn't dare go into a junior high group and say, "That was a *queer* answer" or "This is such a pretty day. We should all be *gay.*" Junior highers have only one definition for those words, and it isn't the one I am using. We simply wouldn't be communicating the same message.

This may be one of the problems with dress and appearance. Although jeans with holes might mean rags and poverty to us, they may have an altogether different connotation to him; so he doesn't understand our hang-up over his holes.

Actually the dress question points up an interesting matter for parents. We need to stop occasionally, and ask ourselves, *Who owns the problem?* If the way your junior higher looks is causing you a problem, you have a right to tell him, "Look, I may be a grouchy old fogey, but we need to understand each other. Let me tell you why I don't like your style; then you tell me why you do. Then we will talk about how we are going to reconcile our differences."

This may not get him out of those worn-out jeans, but that kind of gentle honesty ought to be a bit easier on your ulcer.

9

Hunks and Their Admirers

"At what age is she old enough to date?"

Here comes Carol down the hall, holding hands as usual. This time it's with Rick. A couple of days ago, she was walking arm in arm with Greg. I don't think she's too selective at this point. She just likes boys, and she seems to like having them touch her.

Obviously, her social antics are a real nuisance in the classroom. There is probably nobody as eager for female attention as an eighth grade boy, and nobody as awkward with it. But beyond that, I am worried about Carol. Watching her public display of affection, I shudder to think what is happening privately.

I will accept the argument that physically Carol is more woman than child, and I realize that in some cultures Carol would probably be married and on her way to motherhood by now. But that is not the way it works here. The junior highers might sense that something is unfair about all this—that nature says they are adults but culture says they are children—and this injustice may be a source of frustration for them, but that is the way things are. That is one of the problems of reaching this age. When the junior higher suddenly realizes his power, society tells him not to use it.

Simply stated, Carol is headed for trouble. At this point, I am going to avoid the urge to play amateur psychologist and guess at all the reasons for Carol's cravings. Maybe she is lacking something or looking for something, or protesting something. Regardless of the reasons, Carol's actions are about to lead to some rather serious consequences; and I'm not sure she even realizes that. Although we may not be able to prevent Carol's needs, we can at least teach her how to deal with them.

Carol is in urgent need of sex education. I don't know where she is going to get her training, but she needs it. If she doesn't get a formal study, she is going to get an informal one quicker than we want her to.

I do realize that this is an unpopular subject. Sex education is the real stepchild of child-rearing agencies. Schools may attempt a bit, but their efforts are almost always limited to issues of fact. Some good teachers may teach your child the facts of sex, but the subject is deeper than that.

Although the school attempts are inadequate, studies indicate that parents aren't doing much better. Recent surveys maintain that fewer than 20 percent of high school students have received any sex instruction from their parents. That leaves about 80 percent of the nation's children to learn on the streets or from the activities that follow such things as holding hands in the halls.

In spite of how much I hate such encounters, if Carol were my daughter, I would swallow my pride, argue with my face about turning red at inopportune times, muster my courage, and begin a long series of serious discussions with her. Of course, I just wouldn't blurt it out. I would try to create a tender time—some occasion when she is pleased to be my daughter and when I am pleased to be her parent, some occasion when both of us are feeling good and both of us are acting like adults. But I would get into the conversation soon.

Regardless of whether she gets the information and understanding from her parents or some other source, Carol needs to learn several lessons.

1. *She needs to understand how her body works.* Although I put this first on the list, I do so with some reservation. Unfortunately, most sex education not only starts but ends here. This is about as much as schools or bold parents get into. But it simply isn't enough. The whole business of human sexuality is a complex issue and when your junior higher first discovers it, he or she is going to need some help to understand how it works. You wouldn't deny him food for physical growth. Make sure he isn't shortchanged in this area either.

   But regardless of all other valuable components of sex education, the junior higher needs to understand how the body works, how the impulses affect the body and how conception occurs. These facts are part of the mystery and beauty of God's creation. If the junior higher does not learn about his own body within that framework, he will still make the discoveries—but they will have a different meaning to him.

2. *She needs to understand the moral code.* I always get accused of being a sexist when I make such statements as these, but most junior high males are going to depend on the females to establish the sexual rules. If the girl is willing, the guy almost always is. Carol's hand-holding partners will go as far as she permits them. This may seem like an unfair burden of responsibility to put on the females, but it is there and Carol needs to know about it.

3. *She needs to try to understand her own emotions.* Look! I am a parent, and I would really like to ignore the fact that my teenager is feeling all those emotions connected to an awakening and growing sexuality. I would like to think that she is immune to those—that I have taught her so well that those emotions are somehow counteracted with more important things to think about.

   I would really like to believe all that, but I know it isn't true. So now I must help her understand where those emotions come from and how to live with them.

4. *She needs to understand the consequences of sexual activity outside of marriage.* Anybody who engages in sex at this age is going to inherit a plethora of problems. Carol needs to hear about those.

5. *She needs an honest relationship with a responsible adult.* One of the by-products of a good discussion with Carol could be that the two of you get close enough that she is willing to discuss things with you. At this point, Carol needs that kind of honesty. She isn't mature enough to accept her emotions or their consequences. She needs help in understanding herself, but in order to get it, she needs to feel comfortable discussing herself. Take the initiative and start the relationship.

6. *She needs to realize the biblical mandate to fidelity.* The Bible is filled with texts that teach us this great principle. What you select is a matter of choice.

Personally, when that time comes for me to gulp for fresh air, turn purple, stammer, and perform my fatherly duty of talking to my children about the beauty of sexuality, I start with Ephesians 5. I want to couch the whole discussion in the image of a model love—the love of Christ for His bride, the church.

I hope Carol can somehow catch a glimpse of this kind of total love before she plunges into a relationship that makes a mockery of it.

10
Leaders and Followers

*"Who is this Craig we hear about all the
time—some kind of Pied Piper?"*

As a visitor in the eighth grade class, I sat at the back and
watched the students file in. Although he wasn't really that
different, I picked him out immediately. He was dressed in
the standard costume, and he wasn't any bigger than the average guy. But he came in with an air of assured reserve
which indicated that he knew his role in the class and the
role he had in the lives of many of the students. Almost as if
by ironic design, he took his seat right in the middle of the
room.

The teacher opened the class by reading an e. e. cummings poem she had written on the board. It was a meaningful ditty, packed with imagery and surprise. When the
teacher followed with a question, a large guy sitting over
near the windows came to life. He held up his hand with
that burst of enthusiasm which says, "Call on me, Teach,
I've got a better idea than anybody else." But suddenly, as if
he remembered something, he pulled his hand down and
turned his head so he could catch the leader in the corner of
his eye.

Mr. Assured answered the question himself. With a visible sigh of relief, the large guy by the window lifted his
hand, offered a further point, and took an active role in the
rest of the discussion.

If I were the parent of a boy in that school, the first thing I
would want to know is who is this guy who has so much

power that the other students have to check with him to see if it is all right for eighth grade boys to enjoy such things as a "mudluscious world."

When we talk of peer pressure, we usually think in terms of some kind of nebulous mob agreement. But for junior highers, it may be more complex than that. Often, as in this situation, the source of peer pressure may be one person; and the kinds of attitudes and activities the rest of the people endorse are directly affected by what that one person thinks and does. For the boys in this class, and I suspect for most of the boys in that school, this one young man represented peer pressure.

Leadership intrigues me. It is more of an aura than an act—more charisma than content.

I have no idea how this leader got his position. Perhaps at one time he could run faster than anyone else. Perhaps he was the first kid on the block to have his own Pac-Man game. Perhaps he could beat them in a fight. Perhaps he had style with the girls. Or perhaps he just had a rare combination of hero qualities. Regardless of where he got his power, he wielded a strong hammer over the lives of those students. For the boys in his class, that one young man was the embodiment of peer pressure.

If your junior higher has that kind of hero worship for one of his classmates, your first task is to know who that hero is. Have your child invite him over to the house. Meet him on friendly and frequent terms. You may even call his parents and get together with them on a friendly basis. If this leader is the right kind of person, your junior higher is going to have far less trouble getting through those changing years.

On the other hand, if this leader is the type of person you don't want your child following, you have a different kind of problem. How do you tell anybody that his favorite person is a bum? How do you reason against an adoration that isn't based on objectivity in the first place?

Since you probably can't do much to alter your child's impression of the leader, you have two options. You can take the easy way out and just try to live through the duration. One thing about this kind of a relationship is that it is as fleeting as the junior high years. In a few months, it too will fly away.

But if you feel that you must do something, you may try to work directly with the leader. Again, take the initiative. Invite him into some of your activities. After you get close enough to him, you may earn the right to help him realize the power he has over the lives of others.

In the case I described, this class leader appeared to be worthy of the respect he had achieved. Anybody who shows interest in e. e. cummings can't be all bad.

And he does represent one kind of relationship your child, male or female, is likely to have during the junior high years.

Now, let's look at a relationship at the other end of the scale.

11
Robert: The Human Football

"Now that he is in junior high, he cries every morning before school. Can things really be that bad for him?"

"Johnny, think of an adjective and use it in a sentence showing its three degrees."

Johnny has been waiting all period for this opportunity. "Robert is fat. Robert is fatter than anyone I have ever seen. Robert is the *fattest* person in the whole world."

"And the *laziest*," adds Charles.

"And the *ugliest*, yech!" adds Marie.

"You would be fat too, if you ate like he does," adds another classmate.

Poor Robert, and this is still the first hour. Before the day is over, he will be kicked and punched, his sandwich will be squashed, someone will break his pencil, and he will be pushed off the sidewalk while trying to walk home with some of the "guys." I do feel sorry for Robert, but the person I really feel sorry for is his younger brother when Robert finally gets home after a day of all this abuse.

Robert represents one of the most difficult challenges for a junior high teacher and especially for a junior high parent. Most of the time, junior high people can be very understanding and loving, and even tender on rare and secret occasions. But sometimes, they can be brutally cruel, and usually that cruelty is directed toward one person—Robert in this case.

I am not sure I know how Robert got the office of human football. In some ways he isn't quite as mature as the other students, but he is not really that different. Sometimes he may not be as easy to be around as he could be, but many of these students are capable of childish behavior. Yet, for some reason, Robert has been designated as the morale booster. One of the ways to join the gang and to prove oneself as a thinking human being worthy of membership in the in group is to put Robert down. And to achieve this end, almost anything is acceptable.

Although I don't understand how Robert got elected, I do think I understand the need for the office. I don't approve, but I understand. It seems to me that there is an innate human need for each one of us to feel that we are better than someone else. This attitude may not be scripturally sound, but it seems to be fairly universal. That is why we play football games—to prove to ourselves that we are better.

For the junior highers, this need seems to be particularly acute. Since they are in the process of change, they really don't know themselves very well. Since they are at that awkward age of being too old to be cute and too young to be handsome or beautiful, they don't know for sure how they look. Although they are getting a grip on some adult powers like reproduction, society tells them they shouldn't use these powers. In the midst of all these inconsistencies and contradictions, the junior highers need to reassure themselves that they are all right. So they pick on Robert. Although adults may have politer and more sophisticated methods of convincing themselves that they are superior to someone, most of us still seem to have the need.

But in the meantime, we must think of something to do for Robert. For a teacher, Robert presents an almost unsolvable problem. The English teacher could have stopped that in-class teasing; and had she been forceful enough, she could have made sure that it would have never occurred in English class again. But she could not have made Robert a popular hero, and the students would have just found another setting to persecute him. Besides, her punishing the students for their teasing might have actually made matters worse for Robert once class was over.

Again, the teacher might have tried to make Robert better liked, to have treated the cause and not just the result, but those efforts must be very subtle lest the students see through them and acquire just one more reason to tease Robert.

I suggest the teacher's dilemma as a study for parents. If Robert is your child, you are going to spend some distressing days before the two of you escape the junior high years. Robert is going to be unhappy, and I am not sure you can prevent that.

You might begin by helping him work on his social skills. Sometimes, people need to learn how to be polite and how to take a joke. Or, you might try to channel him into a companionship with someone who will accept him. Or, if the situation is really critical, you may want to give Robert some adultlike experiences or responsibilities that will give him some confidence in himself. These efforts may help, but we can't expect miracles. Once a person gets burdened with Robert's role, it is difficult to escape.

On the other hand, if your child is not like Robert, you may want to keep in mind that there probably is a Robert at school; so you may want to talk to your junior higher about this very thing. The best thing that could happen in this situation would be for one popular person to take Robert's side. If the right junior higher accepted him, that could turn the whole process around. So, you may want to talk to your child about his work as a junior high minister witnessing to the divine nature of every creature.

12
When the Old Gang Expands

"Is it too much to ask that we know who his friends are? After all, there is a good junior high group in our church."

"Dr. Schimmels?" And this guy is a friend. When it starts out this formally, I know I am going to get an opportunity to give some cheap advice. "Could we have lunch tomorrow?"

He had me trapped. I'll go anywhere and give advice on any subject for a free lunch, so I accepted.

The problem was not that unusual. Cary was a normal (if there is such a thing) seventh grader who loved his parents, made good grades, played baseball with the neighborhood kids, and had won five Sunday school medals in a row for perfect attendance. All parents should have problems like that.

Cary had been in junior high about three months, and he was having a blast. Because of the variety of activities, he now had a school setting to incorporate all his talents. He played soccer, sang in the choir, and played in the swing band. Through those activities, he had achieved more attention and popularity than he had been used to having.

But now the conflict. This was the weekend for the church's junior high fall retreat. That was a big deal—three fun-filled days without parents and with the bare minimum of adult interference. Three days given to worshipping, studying, playing childish tricks on each other, flirting, and being flirted with. Since Cary had been so active in the church all his life, he would have been looking forward to his first retreat for years.

But on the night before his father called me, Cary announced that he didn't want to go. The school was having its Fall Mixer on Friday night, and Cary preferred that over the retreat. He had studied the situation and had made a decision. He would rather stay for the mixer with school kids and miss the whole weekend with church kids.

Since Cary was their oldest son, this conflict was a new development for these parents. Always before this, Cary's world and interests were within the scope of the parents' control—family, church, and neighborhood. But now junior high school introduced him to a wider range of interests and people, and some of his old preferences were being redefined.

It wasn't as if his parents didn't trust Cary or didn't trust his judgment. But since he had always been so involved in church acitivities, they had just assumed that this would continue. They liked the idea, but this new development would take some getting used to.

Confidentially, I took the man's free lunch under false pretenses. I am not sure there *is* any right advice in this situation. If you are the parent of a junior higher or someone approaching that age, you may as well prepare yourself. Your child is about to discover a bigger, more inviting world than the one both of you are used to dealing with. And the discovery of this world is going to cause some conflicts. Although your child may continue to be the same dependable, loving child he has always been, that new world will force him into some preferences you might not necessarily endorse.

Perhaps the worst thing we can do in this case is panic. I don't think Cary's decision reflected a desertion of his church or loss of his faith. Rather, I think he preferred his school friends over his church friends, at least for this weekend. It was as simple as that.

Actually, a situation like this could provide parents a good opportunity for a lesson in decision making. This would be an excellent time for Cary and his parents to talk about the two choices, to weigh the pros and cons, and to explore the consequences of such decisions. It is also a good time for the parents to present their biases and preferences in a nonthreatening and nonpunitive way. After all, my children are entitled to know the personal whims that dictate some of my decisions about parenting. So I tell them, "Look! This is my problem and not yours; but since I am the one old enough to have a heart attack if he doesn't get his way, this is how it's going to be for now."

But after all that deliberation, if Cary were still determined in his decision, I would recommend that his parents support him. Take him to the mixer. Debrief him when he gets home. Make sure he knows you are interested in keeping up with that expanding world of his.

Of course, there is a simple answer but a difficult solution to Cary's dilemma. It would be convenient if his church friends and school friends were the same people. It was not until my own children entered junior high that I realized the community nature of most churches; but in every church we have ever attended, there is a dominant school in the youth group. The students who attend that dominant school tend to be more visible throughout the church than those who attend other schools. This was the case with Cary. Since he didn't go to school with most of the youth group, he found more companionship with school friends.

This problem is particularly acute in churches that also conduct Christian schools. The children who attend both the school and the church tend to develop very close ties with each other and the church; but the children who attend the church but go to school somewhere else always seem to be on the outside looking in.

If your child does not attend the dominant school at your church, you may need to prepare yourself for some of the adjustments both of you will have to make when he discovers that bigger world of junior high.

13
Failures, Frustrations, and Delayed Achievements

*"The events of the day can upset her
so easily. What can we do to help?"*

On some days, we debrief during dinner. Doesn't that evoke a nice image? This friendly, happy family sitting around the table, leisurely remembering the events of the day, sharing prayer concerns, stopping occasionally to read a relevant passage from the Scripture. Well, it is a nice scene and at our house we do play it regularly—at least once a month. We have this kind of meal whenever no one has to run off for piano lessons, or no one is late getting home from track practice, or no one has to eat in a rush and get to church for a deacon's meeting, or there is nothing really good on television. As I said, we eat a leisurely dinner at least once a month, even if we have to force it.

Isn't human nature strange? Perhaps the most significant and memorable activity of our family is this unhurried meal, and we can't manage to find the time for it except on rare occasions. But since you don't have this problem with your family, I won't spend any more time on this digression.

"Kris," I asked our seventh grader, "When are you going to hear the results of the musical tryouts?"

"She posted them today."

"Oh?" With junior highers, you sometimes have to use the art of "encouraging listening."

"Yeah, Dianne got the part."

After some silence, I replied. "Well, Dianne will do a good job."

"Yeah. She can sing better than me."

After some meager attempts to relieve the tension I had created, I suddenly thought of something more positive. "How's basketball practice?" *That one ought to change the tone,* I thought.

"Well, she called us in today and said that she would only be able to keep twelve girls."

"Oh?" more encouraging listening.

"I wasn't one of the twelve."

At that moment, I wished I had a deacon's meeting to attend.

Yet, this was one of the most critical nights of our family history. Kris had suffered two major setbacks, both in the same day. Despite her lackadaisical attitude about it and her apparent reluctance to talk about it, Kris had to be suffering emotionally. At this point, parents—even those who feel awkward and useless—were valuable to her. Those setbacks provided us not only a challenge but also an oppportunity. And the opportunity put at least two demands on the parent–child relationship.

1. *We had to help Kris manage her hurt.* To those of us who worry about "important" things, not getting into the musical may not seem too shattering; but for a seventh grader, it may represent all the potential joy in the world. There was no doubt about it. Kris was hurt, and we had to help her manage it.

My first impulse when these things happen to my children (or yours for that matter) is to try to heal the hurt—to kiss it and make the pain go away. This is what I would really *like* to do, but I am convinced that I can't. Kris had suffered some setbacks, and there was going to be some pain. I would worry about her if there weren't. She was hurting, and there wasn't a whole lot I could do to make it go away. Besides, I am not sure that would be the best thing, even if I could. The natural process of growing will inevitably lead to some suffering, and that suffering is valuable in the growing process. Although I don't advocate making children wear leaky shoes and light clothes as some Europeans did, I do think the suffering that naturally seeps into the normal growing process is educational.

2. *We had to help her preserve her pioneering spirit.* Kris had just tackled two challenges. In good faith and with a positive outlook, she had tried to reach into the unknown, to attempt something she had never attempted before. Just to try out for the team and the musical took some courage, some of the experimental bravado that made heroes out of such people as Franklin, Columbus, and William Carey. But both of the challenges had backfired in her face. Her experimental courage had led only to the pain of rejection.

The normal reaction would be to say to oneself, *Oh well, what's the use? I tried and failed. I won't even bother trying the next time.* But this is a dangerous attitude, particularly for a seventh grader. And this may present one of the greatest challenges to parents. Junior highers have to experiment. That is one of the characteristics of the age. But during experimentation, there are always as many setbacks as successes. Somehow, we have to help our children look objectively at the situation, but at the same time, keep enough confidence to keep trying.

That night of Kris's suffering caused us pain too. We had looked forward to seeing her in the musical and we had planned to attend the basketball games. But at the time of crisis, we had to accept our truth and help Kris accept hers.

The one prayer I pray most frequently as a parent (and a teacher) is that the Lord will give me the wisdom to know what to expect of my children. If I expect too little of them, they may waste their creative gifts; but at the same time, if I expect too much of them, I may destroy them with an unrealistic burden.

That night our after-dinner conversation hit on several stories—some from Scripture, some about great heroes, and some about real-life people we knew.

We wondered how Zacharias must have handled the suffering of not being able to speak until his child, John the Baptist, was born.

We tried to imagine the drive that possessed Glen Cunningham to recover from a serious fire injury and go on to become a world-class runner.

We prayed for a young All American athlete, a friend of the family, who had just learned that because of a latent back injury, he would never be able to compete in gymnastics again.

These memories weren't meant to divert Kris's attention from her own hurts; we retold these stories to remind ourselves that we are never the only people suffering. Rather, we used the examples to gain the courage to accept the fact that life is more than speaking and burn scars and gymnastics honors and junior high musicals and basketball. When we have courageous confidence in the truth of the gospel, life always has hope.

I don't know whether Kris learned all that in one night; but at least, there weren't any tear stains on the pillow the next morning.

14
The Appeal and Peril of Older Friends

"But he doesn't seem to like anybody from his school. What's wrong with his having all those older friends?"

"Mr. Shambles?" My name is hard to pronounce, but sometimes these people make more of a mess out of it than it really deserves. Oh well, one of the things we have to learn if we are going to teach or parent junior highers is to distinguish between the big issues and the little ones.

"Mr. Shambles, didja ever see the movie *Porky's?* Man, that's some flick. Ja ever seit?"

"No, Johnny, I am happy to say that I have never seen *Porky's*. But how did *you* see it? It's R-rated and they shouldn't be letting you in."

"Aw, I went with my friends. They all got cards and I just snuck in behind 'em. If you go in with people who have cards, they never ask you. They just think you are as old as your friends."

"How old *are* your friends, Johnny?"

"Mostly in high school. But a couple are already out."

"You mean they have already graduated?"

"Naw. They quit. You can quit when you're sixteen. Really, you can. These guys are pretty neat. They both got good jobs, and they didn't see any need to go to school anymore."

Keep in mind that this conversation took place in the middle of an eighth-grade writing assignment, so it was delivered not only for Johnny and me, but also for the entertainment of the entire class.

Peer acceptance is a tricky business for eighth graders. Some want to be accepted, so they try to look and think exactly like everybody else. Some want to be accepted through the romance of being different from everybody else. But most want both at the same time. They want to think they are unique and exciting, so they tell stories—real and manufactured—to illustrate their sophisticated uniqueness. But all the while, they really want to meet the criterion for peer approval.

Johnny spoke loudly and enthusiastically enough to make sure he was heard and envied by most of his classmates. Johnny wasn't a bad student. In fact, he was fairly bright. He had good learning skills—reading and writing—and he did his work. Despite the rather frequent outbursts of tales documenting the bright-light district of our city, he utilized his time in class efficiently. It was a good thing, though, because I suspect he wouldn't have had too much time to do homework. He was too occupied with his friends—his older friends, who by now not only had decided that homework was not one of the priorities of life but had actually given up on the whole school enterprise.

At this point in his life, Johnny was headed for trouble. It is one thing for a junior higher to get into the wrong crowd, but it is especially dangerous when that crowd is several years older than he. (Remember, at this age, three years is several.)

The problem with this cross-age friendship is that the younger person is always going to be the follower. Johnny wasn't the leader in his group. In fact, he was on the fringe, and deep inside he would have known that. So in order to stay with the group and maintain the privilege of bragging about it in front of the other eighth graders, he had to do what the others wanted him to do. He had to entertain them.

He had to satisfy their need for authority and control in a friendship. He had to respond to their beck and call. He had to slip into the R-rated movies and make the marijuana deals.

His friends were probably thoroughly entertained at Johnny's expense when they bought the beer and got him drunk for the first time in his life. (Remember that these guys had that all-important "card," an I.D. that announces to the world that you have achieved the distinction of being eighteen.) His friends probably arranged and supervised Johnny's first sexual encounter. And for months afterward, they could laugh when they remembered his awkwardness. Johnny might have been having fun, but the older "friends" were the real beneficiaries. They didn't need Rodney Dangerfield. They had Johnny.

At this point, you have probably become a little impatient with me. I am always relating the extremes in these stories. Sure, Johnny is a real person, and the story is believable in that sense. But is it all that universal? Do all these cross-age friendships have to be this earthy?

Of course not! I overdramatize some to make my point, but I do think the essence is there in every case. If your junior high child is running around with an older adolescent, he is not living according to his own moral code. He is living according to the morality of the older friend. If (or when) the opportunity comes for experimenting with alcohol, drugs, sex, dirty books, shoplifting, or joy riding, he won't have the privilege of thinking about whether he wants to participate. That decision was made when he identified with the group.

If you know the older adolescent and have unquestionable trust in him and his judgment, such a friendship may be profitable. Your child could get good moral instruction. If your eighth grade daughter just has to date, you could argue that it would be better for her to go with that nice young sophomore from the church rather than some hooligan her own age. You have a point. But ask yourself first, *Why does that sophomore want to take my daughter out in the first place? Why isn't he interested in a girl his own age? What does he hope to get from this friendship?*

I want to emphasize that young people mature at different rates of speed in different areas. Maturity may be physical, intellectual, emotional, spiritual, or moral. Don't be deceived. A thirteen-year-old may be mature in some areas of his life, but he is still thirteen years old in some others, and a sixteen-year-old is almost 25 percent older than a thirteen-year-old.

Now if I have convinced you of the dangers of having your junior higher in an older friendship, I suppose I have the responsibility of telling you how to prevent it. But as usual, I have more problems than solutions.

Manipulating your child's friendships is not a particularly safe activity itself. I am never sure quite how to go about it. If you don't like some friend selection, your obvious disapproval might be the force that drives them together. So, regardless of how you handle it, you have to be subtle. I suggest prayer, both for yourself and for your child. God promises wisdom if we ask, and I am not ashamed to admit my deficiencies.

Curfew

In some cases, a curfew can take care of some of the problem. Of course, the curfew must be strict enough, and it must be enforced. You have to have the courage to answer the whine, "But nobody else has a curfew. You just don't trust me, and you don't love me either. If you loved me and trusted me, you would let me stay out as late as I want to. Why don't you trust me? What have I ever done. . . ." I throw this in here in case you have heard it recently. I want you to know that it isn't original with your child. It comes off a rather common junior high script. But it sure can make you feel tyrannical when they season it with a little salt water.

But persist. You have logic on your side. People that age simply need more sleep than the older adolescents do. That was one of Johnny's problems. He was staying out too late, and that lack of sleep began to show up in other areas of his life.

Besides, a curfew makes sense from a safety point of view. In this age of rampant and random crime, it is not too much to ask to know where your children are, regardless of their age. I am just arrogant enough to think that if my daughter gets raped, she needs me as quickly as I can get there. At our house, the curfew is for my peace of mind.

If my child has older friends, they will have to bring her home before the party gets in full swing; and they won't put up with this too long.

Activities

Another way to mellow some of those cross-age friendships is to make sure your child stays busy with junior high and junior high people. One of the values of extracurricular activities is that they help the person find an acceptable niche with people his own age. If Helen had been elected cheerleader, her whole experience might have come out differently. Encourage your junior higher to get into things that permit him to earn the respect and friendship of other junior highers.

In fact, if your child is just going into this age, you may need to anticipate. Just remember that everyone needs to fit in somewhere. If he can't make it in his own age group, he may have to try a group above. So you may need to support your child in activities with his own age group.

If Johnny had been the best basketball player in school, he wouldn't have needed the distinction of having older friends. Since he never played basketball, he had to prove himself another way.

Although I never knew his parents, I am sure they would have preferred the inconvenience of supporting his basketball participation over what happened to him as a result of his having to be the clown for his "friends."

With this warning, I conclude the section on the problems of social adjustment for junior highers. I am not finished because I haven't really exhausted all the possible situations that almost any junior higher will encounter.

But my purpose has been to present enough different situations to remind you as an interested (and perhaps concerned) parent that your child, during those years between twelve and fifteen, will meet and deal with a variety of social situations that will bend him, amuse him, challenge him, provoke him, and develop him.

With enough understanding, mutual love, and prayer, you both can make it through this difficult time of junior high life.

Understanding the school structure might also help. So that is the subject of the next section.

15
School: How to Name It—and Why

"What is a middle school, anyway?"

If you are getting confused by all this talk of mood changes, body changes, and social adjustments parents can expect from their children at the junior high age, don't be too dismayed. Other people are just as confused as you are. In fact, even the experts—the educators and psychologists—the people who are supposed to know what this age is all about, sometimes seem a little confused themselves.

Teacher Certification

The whole business of training and certifying junior high teachers is just one example. Although teacher certification varies some from state to state, there are enough similarities for us to make an observation. I will use Illinois as an example.

In Illinois, we have two kinds of teachers—elementary and secondary. Elementary teachers prepare themselves in college by spending a large portion of their time studying teaching methodology. They study how people learn to read, write, and do arithmetic. It is assumed that these people have a sufficient grasp of the subject matter of elementary grades; so to prepare themselves to teach, they need to work on understanding the child and how he learns.

On the other hand, the secondary teachers spend most of

their time studying the content of the field they will be teaching. They major in things like history or English or math, and they take a few courses in teaching theory and methodology. It is assumed that they first must know their subject matter; then they can rather easily learn a few tricks, and they are ready for the next forty years in the classroom.

When the elementary people finish their preparation, they receive a state certificate that affirms their competence to teach grades kindergarten through nine. When the secondary people finish their preparation, their state certificate affirms their competence to teach grades six through twelve.

Now, look at what that says. We really don't know who is supposed to teach grades six through nine! We don't know whether we should turn the education of this critical age group over to elementary teachers specializing in methodology or to secondary teachers specializing in content. Or maybe we should give those students a smattering of both.

In all fairness, some colleges (and even some states) have taken the matter more seriously and are now offering a special preparation program for the prospective middle-school teachers. Nevertheless, most students in this age group are taught by teachers who have not been especially trained for this specific duty.

There is a real paradox here. The basic assumption of this whole book is at stake. I propose that the period of early adolescence is one of the most unusual and most critical periods in a person's development, and wise parents will spend some time preparing themselves especially for the task. Yet, educators themselves can't really decide whether these people at this stage of their lives are at the top end of childhood and should be taught like children or at the bottom end of adulthood and should be taught like adults.

Junior High

During the period from approximately 1835 to 1875, most American children (who had the privilege of going to school) attended the town's school, which housed grades one through eight. In the history of American education, this period is called the common-school movement.

In 1874, the Supreme Court ruled that Americans could tax themselves to support public high schools. Thus, a whole new school level, the high school, was created; and students who graduated from eighth grade went to another building for grades nine through twelve.

In the early 1900s, some schools decided to experiment with this structure; so they pulled grades seven and eight out of the elementary school and grade nine out of the high school and created something they called the *junior* high school. The theory seemed workable from a social and educational point of view. Ninth graders were too young to be in the same building with seniors. Seventh and eighth graders were too mature to be in the same building with all the younger children. The junior high school seemed to be a good solution to several problems.

Educationally, these schools basically tried to live up to their name. In other words, they attempted to be *junior* high schools. They attempted to offer watered down versions of high school courses taught with much the same structure as high school courses. Math teachers taught math, science teachers taught science, and English teachers taught English; and students went from teacher to teacher for an hour a day of specialized study. (This is called departmentalization and is to be contrasted with a self-contained classroom where the students are with one teacher for the whole day.)

Although there were some variations, this structure was dominant for the next fifty years or so. But during the sixties when experimentation was in vogue anyhow, some educators focused their attention on the early adolescent; and they came up with something called the middle school.

Middle School

Although the middle school in its purest form is a rather elaborate theory of education, the movement grew out of discussions of social compatibility of the grade levels of the junior high schools. There is a big difference between the maturity levels of seventh graders and ninth graders. This is immediately evident. So, the educators reasoned, ninth graders shouldn't be in the same building with seventh graders. Seventh graders don't need that kind of influence, and ninth graders need more of a social challenge. Thus, in many school districts, ninth graders were pulled out of the junior high and placed in the high schools. Then, to make the middle school a three-grade enterprise, the sixth graders were brought up from the elementary schools to be with the seventh and eighth graders. Presently, the jury is still out concerning the feasibility of this plan. Perhaps the maturity gap between sixth graders and eighth graders is actually greater than the gap between seventh graders and ninth graders. Perhaps the workable solution would be to have a separate school for each grade level for that age characterized by quick change and extremes. Regardless of the most desirable format educationally, economics will rule out some of my proposals.

Of course, the middle-school engineers and advocates contributed more than a new social structure. They reasoned that these unique people in this age group also needed a unique school experience, one which provided for the students' need for freedom and structure, the need for transition from childhood into adolescence, the need for experimentation, and the need for educational review.

The middle school, then, in its original form, attempted to provide for these needs. Consequently, a large share of the educational experimentation and innovation in the last twenty years has been directed toward the grades six through nine. Despite the continuing confusion about preparation and certification of teachers, educators are still trying to get it right. Just to know that even the educators are working on the problem should be some comfort to parents who are concerned that they don't understand their own child as well as they would like.

To get a closer study of some of these educational theories at work presently, let's look in on three different teachers, each representing a different approach to educating the junior higher.

16
Classroom Innovator

*"It seems to me that they play a lot of games.
Is that outdoor education trip really
necessary? What ever happened to the good
old studies like English and history?"*

Ralph Cowper teaches "eighth-grade core." That isn't a class in apple appreciation; it's a combination of English and social studies. Mr. Cowper's school is generally departmentalized. In other words, the day is divided into seven periods, and the students pass from class to class for most of their studies. But, there is that nagging notion that students this age need a bit more stability. They need some deeper identification with a specific teacher, and they need the opportunity to be with one social group for a greater length of time.

So, in Mr. Cowper's school, that need for stability is met by combining English and social studies into core class, which meets for two periods. Thus, the students have something of a homeroom. They are with their classmates for a block of time. Since the core teachers have only three sections per day, they have an opportunity to get better acquainted with the individual students.

Mr. Cowper himself is an interesting teacher. He is highly educated—having studied overseas in some prestigious programs. He is active in social studies circles and has published papers in social studies and history journals. In the evenings, he teaches specialized courses for one of the local colleges. But Mr. Cowper is a confirmed junior high teacher. He spends most of his time with junior high students. He not only teaches them in the classroom and prepares for his classes at night, but he also supports the junior high activities.

He attends the sports events and musical presentations. He invites junior highers into his home. He counsels with them during lunch and throughout the day. During passing periods, he stands outside his door and calls most of the students by name. Because he is so interested in them and because they *know* he is interested in them, he has earned the right to discipline any student at school. So when a student runs in the hall, Mr. Cowper handles the situation.

In simple terms, Mr. Cowper is a junior high teacher, and he doesn't want to be anything else. He has no false notion of himself as a high school teacher or a college history professor. He understands how junior highers learn, and he likes to teach these people who have some special learning and social needs.

Mr. Cowper's classes are characterized by direction and flexibility. He provides the students with a sense of direction by such little considerations as putting the daily objectives and assignments on the chalkboard. Thus, when the students walk into the room, they glance at the board and know immediately what they are to do that day and what is expected of them. Since they know what must be learned, there is always a bit of urgency about the class, a feeling that the class must move forward because there are important things ahead.

At the same time, Mr. Cowper's scheduling allows for flexibility. This is one of the advantages of the two-hour period. If during a discussion about one topic, some student asks a meaningful question about another topic, Mr. Cowper may have the students gather into a circle and discuss that related topic before they go on with the rest of the lesson. Or if a side topic seems important to a couple of students, Mr. Cowper may assign those two a bit of extra research; and when they have finished, he gives them the opportunity to report to the class. Thus, students have an opportunity to pursue things that really interest them.

Mr. Cowper does utilize small groups frequently. He also uses such teaching techniques as role playing and simulations. In his simulations, the students take a role in a semi-real situation, and they play that role for a while. In fact, one of the major learning experiences of the year is the Model Congress where the students simulate national Congress and play their roles until they have learned how Congress works and laws are passed and implemented.

Since Mr. Cowper knows how a junior high student operates, since he knows about the changes in moods and perspectives, and since he has chosen to teach in junior high, he is not afraid to create situations where the students can feel free to express themselves while they are learning. He gives them frequent opportunity to think, to write, and to present their ideas to class. In other words, he activates the students in the learning process. He accepts their ideas and all their changes; and he offers them consistent support through this critical developmental period. He gives them room to experiment academically; yet, he provides enough direction to keep them in bounds.

Obviously, Mr. Cowper is a popular teacher. His former students drop in to see him and thank him for the direction he provided while they were in junior high school.

Of course, Mr. Cowper also has a supportive administration and administrative policy. The educational theory at his school is that junior high students should be introduced to as many experiences and studies as possible during the seventh and eighth grades. The students in the school take semester-long courses in art, music, drama, shop, and homemaking in addition to their other courses in science and math and the two-course block of core.

Academically, junior high is a period of transition—of transition from the elementary emphasis on learning skills such as reading and writing to high school emphasis on mastering content. Mr. Cowper and his school are providing the students an opportunity to explore themselves, their own minds and abilities, and the world of studies during these transition years.

17
Straight Lecture

*"Why does he say he is bored in class?
I thought he would enjoy history."*

Mr. McCaullay teaches eighth-grade American History. He really didn't mean to, but it was the only job he could get. During his college career, Mr. McCaullay fell in love with history and history teaching. He really got excited about those more informal profs who sat on the edge of their desks and told exciting stories about Civil War battles and heroes with shady personal lives.

Mr. McCaullay decided that he could be happy doing this the rest of his life, so he took the required courses to become a secondary history teacher. Unfortunately, when he finished college, he couldn't find a position with a high school, so he took the job with a junior high.

He told me at the time that it really didn't matter that much. After all, junior high students are only smaller versions of high school students. He could still get excited about making history lectures interesting. He only had to watch out for the big words and cut down on the content a bit. But he could teach eighth grade for a few years, get his feet on the ground, and move into a high school job when one came along.

And now, Mr. McCaullay, in the highest form of praise to his college professors, teaches the eighth graders as he was taught. He sits on the front of his desk and tells interesting tales from the fascinating world of history. His students sit at their desks and practice their skills of listening. Mr. McCaullay, aware that these people are not as astute at hearing as he was, frequently provides them with some listening aids. He gives them outlines to follow or maps to look at, and he does assign readings in the textbook. Those students who are motivated (whatever that means) read the assignments and listen carefully in class. Those students who are not so inclined, listen as best they can while remembering that video games are more fun.

After he has filled so many days with his stories, Mr. McCaullay stops and presents the students with a test to see how much they have heard. Some do well; on the other hand, some don't. Since Mr. McCaullay is a good teacher, concerned about his students, he then provides an opportunity for those who have not done well to try to redeem themselves with another try or extra-credit work. In the meantime, he goes back to telling the history story because he must get through the book before the end of the year. Besides, his favorite period is World War I, and he doesn't want to shortchange that.

Mr. McCaullay's students have learned some important lessons. They have learned to come to class with paper and pencil, and they have learned to sit quietly and attentively.

Unlike Mr. Cowper, Mr. McCaullay does not use oral presentations as a form of instruction. He tried it once, but he found the students to be extremely nervous and incapable of presenting a cogent project. Some of his students actually refused to make a presentation and chose an F for the assignment.

Now, before you get the idea that I am condemning all this, let me assure you that Mr. McCaullay is a nice guy who does care about his students. In fact, some—those who are reserved and intellectual—consider him the best teacher they have. I am glad that he is in the school.

But he does reflect a different attitude and approach to the whole junior high age from that which Mr. Cowper demonstrates. Mr. McCaullay sees the junior high as a time for students to begin to think and act like high schoolers, so he uses the teaching style most common to high school history teaching. He might actually admit, when cross-examined, that the junior high student is different in some ways; but he isn't too happy with that difference, so he chooses to ignore it.

And he and the students go on about their daily business of covering history as he waits patiently until a more important job of teaching high school comes open.

It might be interesting to note that standardized tests, those national exams which tell us how many facts students have catalogued in their brains, will probably reveal that Mr. McCaullay's students are learning about as much history as Mr. Cowper's. This isn't really so startling. In fact, a comparison of types of junior high teachers is valuable to us. It demonstrates the junior higher's resilience and ability to adapt.

18
Same Class; Same Teacher; Same Classmates

"What are the advantages of having her with the same teacher all day? Isn't junior high work too complicated for one teacher to be teaching everything?"

Mrs. Smith teaches eighth grade. "Eighth grade what?" you ask. Eighth grade everything! Everything? Yes, *everything!* Language arts, history, reading, spelling, health, art, drama, music, and even Phys Ed two days a week.

Mrs. Smith teaches what the educators call a self-contained eighth grade. Although there aren't too many of these kinds of classes left and there aren't too many Mrs. Smiths still around either, there are enough to justify our looking into the class and the educational and social theories at work here.

Mrs. Smith teaches in an elementary building that houses grades kindergarten through eight; and in that building, the sixth, seventh, and eighth grades are treated much like the lower grades. At the beginning of the year, students are assigned to a specific section or a specific room or a specific teacher, and they stay with that group throughout the year.

In other words, Mrs. Smith received her thirty students the first day of school, and they spend all day with her except for the hour when they go to a math specialist.

Mrs. Smith, herself, was trained as an elementary teacher, and for the past twenty-five years she has taught fourth grade, fifth grade, and now for the last few years, eighth grade. She teaches her eighth graders much like she taught her fourth graders, except she uses bigger words and more material.

As a veteran teacher, she organizes the school day around a common theme. Each morning, the students begin work on some language arts project—a writing assignment, a short story to read, or a poem to memorize. But then, almost as if in the middle, Mrs. Smith cuts the assignment off and goes on to the social studies lesson. From social studies, the class moves to health, drama, music, art; and two days a week, as the afternoon begins to wear everyone down, the students push the desks aside and venture into some vigorous exercises such as square dancing, aerobic movement, or chair tag to satisfy their need for Phys Ed.

At first glance, a visitor might get the idea that Mrs. Smith's students do not get as much intensified history study as Mr. McCaullay's students do during that one specialized period with him. However, as the common themes keep recurring at odd times, the students probably finish the day with more exposure to the social studies material than they would have had during a specialized period.

Since Mrs. Smith's thirty students are together all day long, they don't have much of a need to build a wide base of acquaintances with a lot of other eighth graders in the school. In Mr. McCaullay's school, his students may be in classes with as many as one hundred different eighth graders during the day. In Mr. Cowper's school, students may have classes with as many as seventy different people. But in Mrs. Smith's classes, these students only need to build friendships with those thirty people.

This helps provide them with a great deal of security. After a few days together, the students form a supportive bond. They seem to enjoy each other. They are not afraid of one another. They have more freedom to be themselves. The shyer and more timid students tend to be particularly happy with this arrangement. There is a general feeling of goodwill and cooperation throughout the room.

This peer security is probably most evident in oral presentations and speeches. As you remember, Mr. McCaullay's students were reluctant to stand in front of their classmates, and Mr. Cowper's students made presentations with some confidence. But Mrs. Smith's students are regular hams. When she gives them the opportunity, they jump at the chance. They are not afraid to let their classmates laugh at them.

Since Mrs. Smith has only thirty students, she knows them well. She might admit that she knows some of them too well. But she does know them. She knows when babies are born into their families. She knows when their dogs die. She knows who has a father; and she know who is running around with the older students. She knows who has friends and who needs friends; and she just might use this knowledge subtly the next time she has need for small group work for an art project.

Overall, Mrs. Smith's students seem to be rather happy to be in her class, and they don't seem to be in too big a hurry to graduate into that foreign world of high school and departmentalization.

"Why then," you ask, "don't we put all junior highers in self-contained classrooms if there is so much security and happiness in that arrangement?"

There are two obvious answers. Some students couldn't stand that much security. They simply need more room and more time. They need the variety of having class with a hundred different people. But the other answer is even more obvious than that. Mrs. Smith's class works because Mrs. Smith is an excellent teacher. She *makes* it work. Students don't naturally come together into a close, cooperative society simply because they are thrown together for most of the day. There has to be some engineering, and Mrs. Smith provides that. Mrs. Smith makes her class.

If those students had a poor teacher, one who didn't care or one who couldn't get the job done, that self-contained class could be devastating.

That's one thing you can say for the system at Mr. McCaullay's school. If a teacher is incompetent, the students only have to tolerate him one hour a day.

I present the descriptions of these three teachers for a couple of reasons. First, I want you to see some of the ways educators are attempting to answer the question, "What do we do with junior highers?" Each of these three teachers is actually quite competent, but each is operating on different theories regarding the general character of junior highers. Although each could probably lodge a persuasive argument for what he or she is doing, they are all guessing. None knows the best way of dealing with all the students. There is simply too much variety in moods, emotions, needs, and maturity levels. Obviously, there is no one right way to educate or to deal with the junior higher.

The second reason I present these descriptions is that I want you to get some idea of what is happening to your child while he is at school, an enterprise that takes up about a third of his day. I would like for you to see the kinds of activities he encounters and the various attitudes of those people who exercise authority over him. By seeing his teachers in action, maybe you can get a better idea of how to complement and coordinate his experience so that both of you can live happily through that time when junior highs invade your home.

The final chapter in this section about schools deals with the most significant (and often the most troublesome) activity of junior high studies—reading.

19
The Reading Problem

*"She never was a really good student, but she
always had a good attitude about things.
Now that she has started junior high, she has
even lost that. What happened to her?"*

Kathy has a reading problem. Actually, it started years ago—perhaps as early as the first grade or maybe even before then. Although the experts project a lot of guesses about why the Kathys can't read, they are still just guessing. Perhaps she has some physiological problem in the way her brain receives signals from her eyes. Perhaps she never learned her phonics. Or perhaps she just never developed an interest in reading so she never worked at it with enthusiasm.

Regardless of the reason, she has a problem. Although Kathy's reading may improve some, her classmates are improving too, so every day the gap between the way she reads and the way they read gets bigger.

Although Kathy had some difficulty in elementary school, she learned to compensate and managed to keep on top of things. She struggled with schoolwork, but she was active and sociable enough to keep strong friendships with the other girls and to participate in normal elementary school activities. She was a part of the group, and she was generally pleased with herself.

But when Kathy entered junior high, that reading deficiency became a real problem with serious consequences.

For one thing, most junior high classwork relies heavily on reading skills. Of course, reading is important for elementary work too, but in junior high most teachers expect the students to read proficiently enough to learn the material through reading. In other words, there is a greater emphasis on reading as a learning tool. Science teachers, social studies teachers, health teachers, and language arts teachers all expect the students to be able to go home and read the chapter for tomorrow's test.

This kind of expectation works against Kathy in two ways: Not only does it take her longer to do the homework, but after all that time, she doesn't get as much out of it as her classmates. Despite the struggling, she still makes lower grades.

Now that Kathy is in junior high, all this has begun to make a difference. If she tries to keep up with her schoolwork, she won't have as much time for social activities; and on top of that, she has begun to lose status anyway. Although rank-and-file junior highers don't particularly like the "eggheads" and "teachers' pets," they still put some stock in being successful. So in junior high there is a stigma attached to the students who struggle academically. Although none of her more capable friends ever make a public announcement of this (in fact, most of them probably don't even know they feel this way), they are very gradually and very subtly turning away from Kathy.

After watching this happen to dozens of girls over the past twenty-five years, I am inclined to believe that there is an even deeper factor involved here. I am convinced that people at this age perceive reading as a feminine activity.

Based on the role models they have observed, they have concluded that reading is a part of womanhood. Mothers read to their babies. While men sit home in their undershirts, drink beer, and watch ball games on TV, women curl up in the corner with a good book or a magazine on child rearing.

So when Kathy reached that age when she came face to face with her reading deficiency and all the subsequent problems, she had to discover another method of self-identity. Kathy chose to try toughness, a fairly common response for junior high girls with reading problems. Early in her junior high career, she started associating with a tougher crowd than she had been used to. Although these are not bad kids, they are on the outside of the mainstream of things, so they try to get attention through techniques designed to shock both their classmates and the adults. They try to look and act grown-up. Their dress reflects this rebellion. And they smoke. Perhaps not everyone smokes; but as a group, they congregate in the vacant lot across the street where they know they are safe from school law.

In class, these students are usually quiet or surly. Since many of them can't read, school isn't much fun for them. Imagine the tedium of spending most of your day being forced to do something you don't do very well. Small wonder they lose interest.

Although there are several reasons why people misbehave in class (and I don't propose to know all of them), I think the people from this group act out for one of two reasons. They either get so frustrated with the situation that they have to rebel, or they act out to protect themselves. A person's ignorance is a very precious and private commodity. I personally go to great lengths to hide my incompetence from anyone I don't respect.

So I am not all that surprised when Kathy makes a real scene on the day we are having students read play parts. She simply doesn't see any need to parade her deficiency out for everyone to see. She can't read—she knows that—but there is no need to show it to the rest of the class.

So she acts out—she talks to her friends, practices her cosmetic skills, or argues with the teacher.

Then we all get the idea that Kathy is a troublemaker; when all the time she is only doing what I do everyday—camouflaging inadequacy. But I don't think we can hope for much success treating the symptom until we get to the disease. And helping a child catch up in reading is a difficult task. But it can be accomplished in most cases. At least it is worth a try.

If your child is experimenting with some unusual forms of social compensation, it is probably worth your time and money to get an accurate appraisal of his reading ability. If your school counselor can't administer the appropriate tests, ask him to recommend a professional tester. If you discover a problem, get help. There are several ways to go about this, but the beginning for all of them is to solicit your child's co-operation and goodwill.

Before bitterness creates a chasm between the two of you, let your child know that you are interested in doing what needs to be done to help him. And ask him for his advice about how you should proceed.

Many junior high schools have a solid remedial reading program, and thousands of people are helped through these. But there are some limitations. For one thing, these programs are not complete within themselves. If your child is going to improve his reading, he is going to have to practice outside school. You can help him by creating the conducive environment and motivation at home, even if it means turning off the TV. Also, far too often, these special reading programs carry a stigma. Nice children read well, but the tough ones don't. Often there is a self-fulfilling prophecy. The people in the special reading programs tend to be the toughest kids in school. If your child is assigned to such a class, you should be alert to this possibility; and you may need to take some action to counteract it. For example, if your child has a talent (such as music) be rather insistent in encouraging participation. He needs some success in any area to help fortify him against the embarrassment of being in the special class.

It probably seems as if I have focused this chapter on a school problem. You want to know how to live with your teenager at home and let the teachers worry about his academic problems. But let me assure you, a junior higher's reading problem will penetrate into every area of his life. If the two of you are going to survive these years, you need to address the issue.

The next few chapters will concentrate specifically on the role of the family in the junior higher's life.

20
When Parents Are a Nuisance

"We try to be nice people. Why does she always act as if she is ashamed of us?"

"But, Daddy, we've just *got* to go tonight!"

"Oh."

"It is going to be a great concert. Our band and orchestra are really good."

"Oh." I am a little cautious about accepting a junior higher's opinion on musical quality. I hear those sounds seeping out of her room.

"All my friends are going to be there."

"Oh." Now we are getting to the real reason, and I suspect she is about to pull out all the big guns.

"Besides, it would be a great family activity. Wouldn't it be fun for the *whole family* to go somewhere together? And what would be better than the school spring musical concert?"

Now, that one makes sense. Families do need to spend time together, and I am encouraged to see her think of her younger brothers and sisters for a change. Most of the time she treats them with an aggressive indifference.

So, after dinner, we load her and the little ones into the station wagon, and travel over to the junior high school for the annual spring music concert. But just about the time we pull into the parking lot, she bolts out the door, runs in, spends the evening sitting halfway across the auditorium from us, and is waiting for us at the car when the whole affair is over. And that is what she calls a family outing.

I don't know whether she is ashamed of us or not. Perhaps we do cramp her style. I guess we are not as romantic or ideal as the movie models. Maybe we do embarrass her. But whether she is ashamed or not, we are definitely a nuisance at this point in her life when she is trying to learn how to fly on her own, to be her own person, to take responsibility for her emotions and actions, to manage her own social relationships. At this point, she really doesn't need interference from us. Besides, to be seen in public with her parents might seriously damage her reputation of independence. In addition to that, having her parents around demands some social graces that don't come easily yet. Just handling introductions can be an embarrassing situation. Trying to remember which person to mention first and then trying to think of the name to use for her parents is worth a giggle or two. When she introduces us to her friends, does she call us Momma and Daddy or the more embarrassing formal titles of Mr. and Mrs.?

Of course, that little show of independence may not be limited to public display. She may even try it out at home occasionally. On the list of things that baffle parents, this is probably number one. Most of the people I talk with simply can't understand that age-old dependent–independent paradox. At one moment, our children are begging us for independence and are vociferously objecting to any parental interference in their lives. Yet, the next moment they come to us with their childlike needs to be filled from the parents' fountain.

Just trying to decide when to hold on and when to let go is enough to drive any normal parent into a state of terminal stress. So maybe the solution is not to worry about it. Perhaps the answer is very simple. We just keep the relationship constant. Despite all her running around to avoid us at the concert, despite all her pleas for her own TV set so she won't have to be in the same room with us, despite all her plans for an "unchaperoned" party at our house, we just keep going on about this business of being parents just as we always have. We won't panic. We won't yell. We won't even demand our rights or threaten her with independence since that is what she seems to want. We will just keep loving her and letting her know that we love her.

In a couple of years—or ten or twenty—she will need us again, and we will still be there. Besides, this concert experience will provide us with a good laugh when she goes through it with our grandchildren.

21
War and Peace: The Sibling Version

*"I am afraid my children really hate
each other. They fight all the time."*

The junior high age is just as paradoxical and unpredictable at home as it is at school. The role anyone plays in the family structure depends on where he fits. To older brothers and sisters, a junior higher is a nuisance—a mere child going through the silliness, awkwardness, and rebellion of transition—someone who lacks the sophistication or opportunity for excitement that an older age offers, so he is always struggling to be something he isn't in order to fit in where he doesn't. At best, he is to be tolerated.

On the other hand, to younger brothers and sisters, the junior higher could easily become a hero. To them, his life does have variety and excitement. When one is ten years old, what could appear more adult and brazen than shifting classes every hour or not sitting with your parents during church or going away on a retreat or buying your very own record for the first time or shaving or wearing eye makeup?

But regardless of the junior higher's family role (somewhere between hero and heel), he is probably confused by it.

Junior high is a time for social adjustments, learning how to manage affairs with a variety of people in a variety of situations; and the relationship with brothers and sisters is just another test.

Despite how special family relationships may be, his re-

sponses to the demands of those relationships will still probably come from within his scope of dealing with any social
problems. In other words, you can probably expect him to
try to manage affairs with his brothers and sisters with some
of the same techniques that he uses with anyone else. Let's
review some of those.

1. Experimentation—Since he is trying to discover what
emotions and feelings are appropriate for everyone he
meets, he needs to try out several. One day, the junior higher
may be cooperative and supportive of a little sister or
brother. The next day, he may ignore the same person. One
day he may admire an older brother or sister. The next day
he may attack that same person with painful verbal darts.

2. Cruelty—Not all junior highers are cruel and no junior
higher is cruel all the time; nevertheless, cruelty is a rather
common technique in some relationships. Junior highers use
cruelty as an expression of frustration and as an attempt to
achieve some self-distinction. Don't be surprised if your junior higher tries a little cruelty while dealing with his siblings,
regardless of whether they are older or younger than he is.
But just because you understand why he tries that method
doesn't mean you have to approve of it. If you don't like his
cruelty, put a stop to it. But try to avoid using cruelty to attack cruelty.

3. Isolation—Often, the junior higher finds relationships
outside the home more fulfilling than those inside the home.
You may not understand that. You might think you are
doing everything possible to make sure he knows he is loved
and cherished. In fact, you may get the idea you are a bad
parent and that you should increase family activities and rit-
uals in an attempt to deal with his rejection of you. But it
may not be necessary. If the bonds and activities that hold

your family together are not as strong as they need to be, I encourage you to strengthen them, regardless of your children's ages. But there is no need to panic just because the junior higher spends all his time in his room behind a locked door. He probably needs some privacy, and we should respect that. Again, I think that as parents you have a right to maintain family functions during his period of personal adjustment. You have a right to demand that he eat meals with the family, take family trips, and do his chores. You can insist that he maintain his family position yet still give him his privacy.

There is a note of promise, though. Usually, the glue that holds families together is like cement. Once it is set and allowed to dry, it gets better with age. When my children were in junior high, I thought that I could be a successful parent if I could just manage to keep them from killing each other; and I knew they would never speak to each other again once they had flown from the nest. But now that they are young adults, they are close friends, cherishing each other's company.

I think the key for parents is to make sure we keep spreading the family glue, even though the splits seem wide and permanent.

22
Getting Them There on Time

*"Now that your children are in junior high,
how do you manage to fill all your spare time?"*

"Now, Mother, let's make sure you've got it straight. I'll
stay after school for cheerleader practice. But you will need
to pick us up at four thirty and take us to the library so we
can work on the science fair project. Then, at seven when
you come to the library, bring a sandwich with you, and I'll
eat it on the way to church for the youth sing."

The junior high experience helps broaden the vocabulary.
Both children and parents learn the operational meaning of
such words as *schedule conflict, priority,* and *choice.* Junior
high is that awkward, in-between age when the people are
old enough to be involved, but too young to provide their
own transportation.

Actually, for most young people, junior high represents a
time for a much wider assortment of activities, and their
participation does put demands on the family structure.

As I stated in earlier chapters, some of this variety is characteristic of the age. Junior high people need to experiment—
they need to find out what their strengths and interests are;
and to do this, they need some participation. As parents, we
have to accept that, despite the inconvenience.

Participation does provide a vehicle for some healthy
learning experiences; yet going into junior high is a bit
like going into the doughnut store. You simply can't have
everything. Sometimes in life we have to make some

choices. This process of choice is easier for some than others. At this age, the more mature are usually the more gifted; so they are in heavy demand. All the coaches and all the directors solicit their participation. On the other hand, the less mature usually have more free time. (And that is an interesting paradox in itself. Although the purpose of participation in an activity is to help the young person mature, the more mature people get more opportunities to mature.)

Regardless of how active your child is, any participation in activities that places him in wholesome contact with other junior highers is important to his development. But participation does affect more than the child. It puts demands on the whole family structure.

Although I am a strong advocate of parental support of the child's participation, the junior higher is old enough to realize that there are other people in the family. And he is also old enough to realize that schedules are coordinated days in advance. In other words, I do not think parents have to be tyrannized by their own children. If your junior higher calls home and says, "Mom, you've got to drop what you are doing and come and take me to play practice because I forgot to tell you," you are not a bad parent if you respond by saying, "No way. You will ride the bus home as we planned. I have had my day planned for a week, and your schedule will just have to fit into mine."

Of course, there will be a little pouting and maybe even a little shouting if your junior higher tends to be bold. But stick to your guns. You have just taught a human being one of the most important lessons he will ever learn. You have taught him that a time schedule is not a matter of life and death, and that other people are as important as he is.

23
Divorce and Its Fallout

"What effect will our divorce have on our junior higher?"

Mitchell and I became close friends. Since he was quarterback of the seventh-grade football team, we had to spend time together (you know the bit—the player has to think like the coach); those times became precious for both of us. We liked each other. We had some of the same values. We enjoyed each other's sense of humor. We appreciated each other's commitment to duty. Mitchell was a very mature, responsible, well-adjusted seventh grader who was fun to be around—the kind of boy who had to be a source of joy for his parents.

After football season, though I only saw Mitchell during class and occasionally in the halls, he was still one of my closest friends. But as winter wore on and both of us got busy, our relationship waned some. I did notice that Mitchell wasn't as jovial in class as he had been, and some of his work wasn't as good as I expected; but I attributed that to snow depression. (As a native Southwesterner, I can understand such things.)

My first cause for alarm came in mid-January. I was called into the office to help the principal with a delicate matter. Mitchell had been caught fighting in the bathroom. Instead of meeting the witty, easygoing, controlled young man I had grown to appreciate, I discovered a calloused, angry person. I could tell that this wasn't a passing mood. Very subtly, there had been a change in his personality, almost a reversal. I decided to interfere, so I called his father. A couple of days later, we met and the father told me about the separation and impending divorce. Recognizing my relationship with Mitchell, his father asked for my help during this difficult period, and I promised to do what I could.

But as soon as the father reported the conversation to Mitchell, I lost my best friend. That boy sat in class and glared at me. When I turned my back, he made snide remarks under his breath; and he approached his assignments with an apathy that looked like resentment.

What had I done to him to earn that kind of treatment? I had entered his secret temple. I had discovered his vulnerability. I knew something about him that he was trying so hard to hide. I knew the source of his frustration, and he hated me for that.

Some writers have projected the idea that the children are somehow made to feel responsible for the breakup of the marriage. I don't know whether Mitchell felt responsible or not, but he definitely felt the stigma. He felt unclean. He tried his best to hide the fact that he was now one of those statistics—a child of a broken home.

I think the hurt went even deeper. Mitchell's father had projected a positive image in the community. He was a leader in business and in his church—a man to be respected and to be looked up to. In fact, he had played the game of fatherhood according to all the rules. He was a faithful supporter of Mitchell's activities. He made sacrifices to attend ball games. He seemed very interested.

Yet, he decided to leave the home and the family. At a time when Mitchell was trying to define the meaning of being a man, the one man he had decided to use as a model deserted him. That vacuum once created had to be filled with something.

Well-informed people have written some excellent books

on the children of divorce, and I won't propose to exhaust the topic in one short chapter; but the subject is relevant to the junior high age. Since the junior higher is already confronted with so many changes, any change in the stability of the family structure will have tremendous effect on him. I don't think we can predict how the junior higher will respond, but he will react in some way.

I am not trying to be preachy here, but I am emphatic. In all my years of dealing with other people's children as a teacher, coach, or principal, I have never seen a divorce that had a positive effect on the children, regardless of the problems of the marriage.

If your children are of junior high age, I urge you to think about the consequences of your actions on their development before you make any decisions to alter the family structure, whether that means separating, getting a divorce, or altering family roles.

For another look at this, let's see it from one girl's point of view in the next chapter.

24
Mothers and Daughters: When the Roles Fit

"She's not just my daughter. She's my best friend. Isn't that neat?"

I had kept Prissy after school—detention, it's called. She had committed some forgettable breach of etiquette which, at the moment, I thought deserved some attention. Since she didn't protest any more than was necessary to keep her image with her classmates and supporters, I concluded that she thought I was accurate in my assessment.

She reported with her books and started to study. I took advantage of her academic bent and went down to the library. When I got back to the room, she was crying. Since she had been almost agreeable about the detention, I decided it couldn't be the punishment that was upsetting her, so I pried.

Prissy told me a disturbing, but far too common story. Her mother and father had recently gotten a divorce. Mother immediately reentered dating activities, and occasionally brought men to the house for the evening. Since Mother needed someone close to communicate with, she enlisted Prissy in the role of companion, consultant, and even confessor.

There were some immediate rewards in that new role. Prissy got some new, grown-up clothes, and she got some good instructions about such things as makeup, men, and flirting.

But now, Mother had become something of a difficult child. She was staying out late at night, and sometimes, she wouldn't come home at all. All this began to frighten, embarrass, and anger Prissy; so, when she thought about it in my detention hall, while she was being punished for some serious crime like chewing gum, she began to cry.

This is a critical situation for any junior higher. Prissy simply couldn't handle the role of child and mother at the same time. For a while, being an equal with Mother seemed like a good deal; but in order to get there, she had to give up her right to be mothered. And she just wasn't ready for that. At a time in her life when she was trying to discover her own role, she was faced with too many options. At a time when she was trying to discover what it is to be a grown-up woman, she found herself in competition with her own mother.

Although I tell this story as a biting reminder about what can happen in a divorce situation, it also has a point for the rest of us. Most junior highers are simply not mature enough and not stable enough themselves to assume the additional burden of rearing their parents too. In other words, junior highers need parents who are old enough to handle their own adjustments.

Let me illustrate. If you come to your son's basketball game and don't like the referees, try not to act childish about it. If you have a disagreement with the way a teacher is dealing with your child, make sure your child knows how you plan to deal with the situation before you embarrass him.

Perhaps the greatest psychological need of a junior higher is the need for mature people as models. At the time when these young people are breaking away from childhood and flirting with adulthood, they need someone to show them what being an adult means. These models are a must for the junior highers. They are going to find them somewhere. If it's not parents or teachers or someone assigned the role by office, they will probably resort to modeling an older adolescent. And this always carries a risk.

Despite all the flack you may get for wearing something gross like wing-tip shoes or jeans without the right label, and despite all the inattention you are going to get when your junior higher is in the company of his compatriots, don't be deceived. He still needs a mature, responsible adult for a role model. He doesn't need a competitor nor a defender. He needs to see how a mature person looks at the world and deals with problems. He needs a *parent.*

25
Dares, Defiance, and Drugs

*"I'm scared to death of drugs. How
do we keep her from them?"*

Lisa would never think of taking drugs. All her life she
has been bombarded with accurate information documenting the perils of drugs and the consequences of drug
use. Since she is a sensible girl, she has made a firm commitment to keep her body free of anything that can cause
that much damage. She may be at the experimentative age
when she will try about anything, but she won't try drugs.
The risk is just too great.

Besides, taking drugs is not a very acceptable activity in
Lisa's crowd. Lisa is a popular student, involved in several
school activities, and she cooperates with the teachers and
makes good grades. None of the people she knows well are
into drugs. They leave that sort of thing to the people who
have already begun to show some disappointment with
life—the people who don't like school activities and classes.

During the spring of her seventh grade, Lisa spent the
night at a slumber party with three or four of her friends. As
the evening wore on and the girls began to get silly through
sheer exhaustion, they decided to make things exciting by
experimenting with some tricks they had heard about. They
began with trying to pass out by breathing deeply ten times
and then having someone push the rest of the air out. After
this game didn't produce any great, earthshaking results, the
hostess proposed another measure. Since the family was
asleep, she would sneak into her father's liquor supply and

get something for them to drink. Through stifled giggles, they executed the crime, and each girl drank enough alcohol to begin to feel a bit woozy. This little ordeal provided them with embarrassment and chuckles and grown-up secrets for the next couple of weeks.

But when the group planned the next slumber party, they all naturally assumed that liquor would be a part of it. It had been so much fun the time before, and it had all seemed so innocent. What harm could come from this? Besides, a couple of girls had watched their parents drink in the meantime, and they were eager to demonstrate what they had learned about the art.

This is how it all started—at a slumber party, but this little band of girls had now been introduced to alcohol. It soon became a part of their social activity; and by the time they were in the middle of the eighth grade, Lisa and her friends were finding some opportunity to get tipsy as often as once every two weeks.

Lisa had a drug problem.

I didn't mean to trick you with the title of this chapter, but I did intend to shock you. When I talk with parents, I sense a rather universal fear of drugs. Parents, and I am included in this group, tremble at the mention of such words as *marijuana, LSD,* or *cocaine;* and we all want to know how we can keep our children away from these dangerous elements. If you are worried, I don't blame you. I am worried too. Junior highers do get into drugs, and your child may be one of them. But if this is a possibility, you need far more information than I can provide in one short chapter. See a counselor. Get help.

I also want to shock you into seeing another point. While you are spending so much of your time and energy trying to protect your children from "drugs," don't forget how easy it would be for them to get introduced to alcohol. And don't forget that alcohol is a drug—that it is, in fact, the most widely abused drug in the country and the most common drug among junior highers.

Those junior high educators who care about their students' personal lives and worry about how the junior highers spend their time, consider alcohol use as the most urgent concern for school people and parents alike.

For one thing, alcohol use is so widespread because it is easier to get. If Lisa were getting tipsy on cocaine as often as she were on alcohol, someone would know it fairly soon. That kind of habit would soon play havoc with the weekly allowance. However, she *can* find the alcohol—in friends' liquor cabinets or at beer parties. Somewhere, she will get the opportunity.

For another thing, alcohol seems to some junior highers to be a safe experiment; and as I have said before, junior high is a time to experiment. Lisa is a sensible girl. She would not intentionally harm herself. She and her friends were not reacting against anybody or anything. They were just experimenting with a new experience. And surely, they reasoned, that experience can't be too dangerous. They know a lot of nice people who drink occasionally. So when they got to that age when they wanted to try a little different zing in life, alcohol seemed to be a reasonable and safe choice.

At this point, you may ask, "Yes, but is alcohol really as dangerous as the other kinds of drugs that we worry about? Are we making too big a deal out of a bit of innocent drinking?"

Well, I don't want to get into any argument that would require comparing the dangers of one high against another, but there are enough facts about teenage alcohol use to frighten me. There are enough facts to convince me that I don't want my fourteen-year-old at the stage where Lisa was during her year in eighth grade. Let me list some of those facts.

1. *Alcohol is addictive.* That is an easy point to document.
2. *Alcohol dulls the brain and impairs judgment.* With as many challenges as life itself presents to junior highers, they don't need the added burden of going into any experience half-armed.
3. *Alcohol relaxes social inhibitions.* During this age of experimentation, when the junior higher is trying to develop his own moral code and test the fences, he really doesn't need any foreign substance to give him a false sense of courage. Many seem to have too much of that already. When my child gets to the point of making some decisions about what he will or will not do, I want him to remember clearly everything I have ever taught him about how to behave.
4. *Alcohol use often has unpleasant consequences.* There are too many stories of tragic automobile accidents for me to ignore the dangers of teenage drinking. When those people involved are only facts in the newspaper, we tend to be rather philosophical about the whole thing; but when someone we know is injured or killed, we suddenly realize that teenage drinking does destroy the lives of some very precious people.

In my years as a teacher, I have lost some of my closest friends through teenage drinking bouts. That is why I am so worried about Lisa.

If I have convinced you that alcohol use is a potential danger for your junior higher, I have achieved my major goal in this chapter. I want you to think seriously about that possibility, and I want you to think about what you can do to help your child through this period of temptation. For that mission, I do have a few suggestions. These may not be applicable in all situations, and the list may not be comprehensive enough to cover all possibilities; but at least you will have some vehicle of action through which you can direct your concerns.

1. *Know when your child first uses alcohol and every time he uses alcohol.* I like giving advice. It is so easy. Notice how I can just matter-of-factly make that statement. Now it's your problem to decide how to do it. But I am serious. If you are really concerned about your child's relationship to dangerous drugs and you truly want to be instrumental in his decisions about them, you are going to have to know your child. You are going to have to have a good enough relationship with your child that you will know when he is experimenting. You are going to have to have a good enough relationship that the two of you can be honest with each other. This is the key. There aren't any shortcuts. There aren't any easier ways. If you don't have such a relationship, find the time to establish one.

2. *Present the facts about alcohol.* As I said at the beginning of the chapter, the distribution of information concerning the dangers of drugs seems to be having some effect. After so long, people do respond to the facts. Give your child the facts about alcohol, but make sure you are telling him the truth.

3. *Show your child how to live a happy, pleasant, fun-filled life without alcohol.* There are enough sources around showing him the alternative. He sees that on TV, or in his friends, or even in his sports heroes. But as you show your child how he can manage his life without artificial highs, you must remember that he is at the age when he demands that advice be based on commitment. Let me put this into a question: Would you be pleased if your junior higher had the same attitude toward drinking as you do?

In fact, as I conclude this section of chapters on the role of family in the junior higher's development, this question, paraphrased and generalized, becomes a theme. As my own children grow older, I am beginning to realize the validity of some of the biblical promises regarding child rearing. If we teach right with words and deeds, if we pray faithfully, and if we are patient, God has promised to regard those efforts. Will you be pleased if your child lives his life according to what you have taught him?

You may ask that question as you read through the final section, which deals with junior high interests and activities.

26
Heroes: Worship or Direction?

"Whom is he trying to imitate this time?"

A mother called me. She was more amused than concerned. Her son, a popular eighth grader, had developed the strange habit of standing around tossing a fifty-cent piece into the air. When he talked on the phone or stood around at home or waited at the store, he would whip out his well-worn half-dollar and flip it.

Observing this, the mother was rather amused until some of his friends came over to spend the night. They were also flipping half-dollars. How did this new fad get started?

That was an easy question. Early in the year, one of the veteran Phys Ed teachers was hospitalized, and we replaced him temporarily with a young professional baseball player who was between seasons. The baseball player was everything an American hero should be—athletic, good-looking, and rich enough for a young man. Besides, he had the romance of stardom. And he had one interesting habit. You guessed it. He stood around flipping a half-dollar. Considering the role he played in the lives of our kids, I am surely glad he didn't chew tobacco.

But that mother pointed out something valuable for all parents and teachers: junior highers are imitators. Heroes are important to them because they need models; they need examples; they need someone to show them the way. Whether he realizes it or not, the junior higher is in transition. Somewhere between the ages of twelve and fifteen, he is going to have to surrender much of what he believes and thinks and needs, and he is going to have to accept a whole new set of postulates for living his life. He is going to have to leave childhood and look toward adulthood.

To make that transition, he has to study life-styles as they are actually lived. He has to have role models. He has to have heroes.

Thus, one of the ways to begin to understand your child is to learn something about his heroes, those people he admires. The most efficient way to discover that is to ask him. Find the proper moment and ask him. In fact, this isn't a bad game to play at home with the whole family. Call in the brood and have them write down the names of the three people they most admire. The answers may startle as well as educate.

Many of my teacher friends survey the junior high students every year, and the responses fall into a fascinating pattern. Let's see if you can guess.

Rank the following classes of heroes the way you think the junior highers ranked them most frequently in confidential surveys.

____ Family members (parents, grandparents, older siblings)
____ Peers (other junior high students who are well-known for some reason)
____ Teachers
____ Publicized figures (entertainers, athletes, politicians)

Would you believe that junior highers select their heroes just as they are listed above? An overwhelming majority select a family member as their first choice of a hero or the person that they most admire. Are you surprised? Frightened? Elated?

Given the role that heroes play in the lives of these people, and given the results of these nonscientific surveys, this does make the junior high years a critical time for parents as well as children. Not only do we need to concern ourselves with how our children are making it through the transition, but we need to concern ourselves with what we are actually showing them to help them through the trip.

27
Thieves and Other Excuses

"He said he got a C because somebody stole his homework. Is that possible?"

The first thing you must learn if you are a teacher or a parent of a junior higher is that they never lose anything. I know that for a fact. I coached junior high sports for five years, and I never once had a player lose a single piece of equipment.

But stealing is a different matter. They "steal" from each other all the time. In fact, I heard the following conversation so often I can recite it in my sleep. Just fill in any name. Your own junior higher's might be appropriate.

"Coach, somebody stole my sweat sock."

"What?"

"Somebody kiped my left sweat sock!"

"How do you know it was your left sock?"

"Because it is the one I always wear on my left foot."

"You mean your sock is shaped to fit your foot? How long since you washed your stuff?"

" 'Bout two weeks."

"You mean to tell me that somebody stole a sock that had two weeks of your crud on it?"

"They sure did. I put my socks in my locker last night and locked it. Now, when I get here, the left one is gone. Somebody stole it and when I catch him, I'm going to sue." (See how sophisticated they have become recently?)

The thing that startles me about this conversation and the

thing it took me years to learn is that this person is serious. In his perception of the situation, someone *stole* his sock. After all, he is a responsible person. Almost every day he puts his socks in the locker. He has a mental recollection of doing it day after day, and he can't believe that yesterday was an exception. So the only logical conclusion is that someone stole the sock. This is the way it has to be. How dare me accuse him of being forgetful or careless! He is in junior high. He is old enough and adult enough to handle responsibility. Forgetting is for children, and I should recognize his maturity.

Illustrations of this junior high attitude are common enough to suggest an epidemic. Yesterday I visited a school to witness a schoolwide locker cleanup. A girl had reported her book stolen, so the principal decreed that every locker would be cleaned and all books would be checked. This morning the principal told me that the girl later found her book at home.

In this morning's paper, there was a story of a teacher being sued for ordering a strip search of seventh graders. A student reported his small calculator stolen, and the teacher ordered his classmates searched. The student later found his calculator where he had left it—in his book. Of course, the teacher shouldn't have conducted the search, but it does seem sad that he is in all this trouble over a calculator that wasn't really stolen after all.

Perhaps the reason we adults get ourselves in trouble helping these people is that they are so convincing. They believe what they report. There is no way it can be any different from the way it is reported. We have no alternative but to believe them and take appropriate action.

I suppose I ought to conclude this chapter with some practical suggestion for dealing with this problem, but I don't have one. I am just reporting it. It exists and it is typical of the age.

I think the mistake in perception grows out of the junior higher's need for respect for his maturity. I recognize that need, and I am willing to work with it. But it sure can be a nuisance sometimes.

28
The Plight of Being Bright

*"He is so bright, and we are proud of him.
But sometimes he does get on our nerves
with all of his knowledge. We wonder how
the other students feel about him."*

As a visitor in the eighth grade class, I noticed Richard as soon as I walked in. He was lean and intense, and he wore horn-rimmed glasses. But I think the giveaway was the fact that he had buttoned the top button of his sport shirt.

As soon as I could, I worked my way around to him to see if I could discover what lurked behind those horn rims. I decided to check on his reading material as an opener.

"Is that a science fiction book you are reading?"

"Yes, it is."

"You must like science fiction." (It was a lucky guess. Horn-rimmed eighth graders usually like science fiction.)

"Well, actually, I prefer fantasy."

"Oh, anything in particular?" I was more than curious. I was actually getting in over my head, and the fact-finding tour had just turned educational.

"J. R. R. Tolkien is my favorite. I read the Trilogy last weekend and found it totally delightful."

At this point, the girl assigned the seat next to Richard ventured her opinion of our conversation. "Oh, shut up," she said convincingly and disgustedly.

Richard reached under the desk, kicked her soundly, and went back to the world of Ray Bradbury and imagination.

Richard is fun. Having him in class is a bit of a test because he sometimes wants to make big deals out of minor points—those points his colleagues failed to remember. He still enhances the discussion, and he challenges the adults around him. But at the same time, Richard's junior high life is not always all that rosy. Actually, his problem is similar to Helen's of the earlier chapter. Where she matured physically before her time, he is simply growing up intellectually a little early. Where she had an adult body struggling against a child's emotions, he has an adult mind struggling against a child's emotions. As you remember, Helen had trouble winning acceptance because she looked too adult. Richard has trouble gaining acceptance because he just can't keep from sounding adult, at least to the other eighth graders.

Actually, the eighth graders have an interesting love-hate relationship with him. They tend not to like him too much, particularly when he sounds so pompous; but they don't mind having him around when they need help with their homework. Of course, the low-motivated students don't find him acceptable at all. They either ignore him or ridicule him, but Richard is smart enough to stay clear of them as much as possible.

As intellectuals go, Richard is actually in better shape than some others. In addition to being intelligent, he is also gregarious enough not to be ashamed of the fact. It doesn't seem to bother him that he knows the answer when no one else does; and Richard finds delight in being able to share his knowledge with any perspective listener.

Think for a moment about the junior higher who is not only intelligent but shy. That poor child is destined to spend some lonely moments before he reaches an age when knowledge and wisdom count for something.

Despite all the appearance of self-sufficiency, Richard and his fellow intellectuals may need more adult understanding and association than some other junior highers. There are actually two goals here. We want to make sure that Richard isn't lonelier than he needs to be, and we want to give him enough encouragement and stimulation for him to keep developing his mind.

School may not provide all that. I don't mean to shock anybody with that statement, but the educators know it is true. School is not designed to challenge the Richards. In recent years, some junior highs have been rather creative in adding programs for the "gifted" which are good at encouraging the better-than-average student. But these programs are still not going to meet all of Richard's needs.

After all, it isn't all that much fun to read Tolkien's Trilogy unless you can discuss it with someone. Richard needs someone to help him satisfy his curiosity and to make him feel good about his natural assets.

If you have a Richard at your house, his junior high years may be fun for you; but you do need to realize his specific adjustment problems. One way to help him through is to make sure that he is included in some adult discussions, and Richard would probably be willing. If you and your adult friends do not discuss the things that interest Richard, you may have to make a special effort to find him discussion friends. You may need to get him into a special study program or a library group. Of course, there is a hazard. Although Richard reads and in some ways thinks like an adult, he is still emotionally thirteen or fourteen years old. That contradiction can be deceiving at times because the adults don't quite know how to relate to him either.

In fact, that is a problem in helping Richard select his reading material. Some great literary works are to be read with the intellect; but some are to be read with the emotions; and Richard is not all that grown-up emotionally.

The interesting paradox with Richard is that while he needs some intellectually mature stimuli, he also needs the activities of a junior higher. So you may find yourself taking Richard to the library's great books discussion one evening and to the roller-skating party the next. Isn't it fun!

29
Poetry and Similar Nonsense

*"I thought I explained it so clearly, but he
asked the strangest questions. It seemed like
I was never going to get it through his head.
What does a junior higher understand?"*

The teacher read the poem:

> Flower in the crannied wall,
> I pluck you out of the crannies,
> I hold you here, root and all, in my hand,
> Little flower—but *if* I could understand
> What you are, root and all, and all in all,
> I should know what God and man is.
>
> ALFRED LORD TENNYSON

Then anticipating a great discussion, she looked up from the book and phrased the first question, "Now, class, what do you think the poet means when he speaks of the wall?"

One young man answered for the whole eighth grade. "He means a wall."

"No," she protested ever so gently, "let's go deeper with this. Let's get beneath the words he used. What do you think he wanted the wall to stand for?"

"How do you know he wanted it to stand for anything? Maybe he was just talking about a wall." His classmates nodded their approval.

"No," the teacher was trying to hide her exasperation. "I

think he was trying to say something else. To say something deeper."

"Well, why didn't he say it then? Everybody is always talking about how poets are trying to say this or that, and it seems to me that if a person wanted to say something, he would just say it outright. How can we expect to know what he was trying to say unless he tells us?"

At this, the teacher closed the book and dreamed of life in the South Seas. Unfortunately, her college professors had forgotten to tell her about eighth-grade reasoning when she was preparing to be a teacher.

But that student and all his supporters weren't trying to be anti-intellectual. They were just trying to see the world from their point of view. Just about the time they were beginning to understand the surface world, someone was trying to tell them that there is a whole other world beneath that structure. They decided to protest that prospect until they could get a better handle on things.

I offer no prescription here—just the information. But all of us who deal with junior highers need to remember it. Psychologists tell us that we should be able to expect a person to move from concrete thinking to more abstract thinking during his junior high years—to move from number lines to mathematical formulas, from walls to symbols. But as we live our lives as models to them and as we talk of truth, justice, and fairness, we need to realize that they tend to see and understand things at the most obvious level.

30
The Fourteen-Year-Old Defense Attorney

"She is always arguing with us or correcting us. Is that typical for a girl her age?"

"Sally, I don't care if you were absent yesterday. You will have to take the test today. You have known about it for two weeks."

"You can't do that," yells out Karen from across the room.

"I beg your pardon." Here I am trying to have a quiet conversation with Sally and I find myself debating someone else.

"It isn't fair. She wasn't here yesterday," Karen continues.

"But she knew about it for two weeks." *Why am I defending myself to this spectator?*

"It still isn't fair. I think she should be permitted to go to the library today and take the test tomorrow." By now, that young barrister had convinced the jury, and twenty-five heads are nodding assent while I stand there wondering how I got tricked into an open debate in the first place.

Perhaps it would make sense if Karen were Sally's best friend, but she isn't. I am not sure the two even speak to each other. Maybe it would make sense if I thought Karen didn't like me, but I think she does. We have nice conversations, and she does good work with a minimum of complaints. So what is the issue?

The issue is actually quite simple for junior highers.

147

Karen has reached the age when she can't tolerate injustice. As a rather intellectually mature eighth grader, she wants things to make sense. She wants people to treat each other according to the rules of human decency. She wants logic and justice to prevail. Since she didn't think I was being logical in Sally's case, she, with her duty to justice, was called upon to champion the underdog. On another occasion, she might have supported me against the students, even if her stand made her unpopular; but this time, she thought I was wrong.

Although I can understand how Karen might be a nuisance at home at times, she is fun to have around. It is refreshing to see a person at any age embrace this duty to justice; but it is rather typical with junior highers.

Of course, their approach to justice sometimes comes equipped with a couple of interesting characteristics that in some ways make it even more charming.

For one thing, junior highers like their justice to be simple and pure. They don't seem to be too interested in the complexities of compromise. Right is right, and that is the only thing that matters.

But at the same time, the junior higher's sense of justice is often a bit egocentric. He first wants to make sure he is treated fairly, and then he may have time to worry about his peers. After that, he may be able to handle some concerns for a bigger world.

I include this description of junior high justice for two reasons.

First, I want to remind you that for the first time since your child was born, you may have to include the reason for every piece of instruction. Junior high is the age when the person wants to know the why of every action and decision. Second, I want to prepare you for some of the questions you may have to answer during those wonderful years when your child is in the process of putting away childish outlooks and speeches. Do you have an answer for any or all of the following?

1. You said we would go tonight. Why have you broken your word?
2. Why do I have to have a curfew just because my older sister stayed out too late when she was my age?
3. You said I could paint my nails any color I wanted and I happen to like chartreuse.
4. Why doesn't the president just cancel welfare and make all those people go to work?
5. If *you* can buy a Fuzzbuster for the car, does that mean *I* can cheat on tests so long as I don't get caught?
6. I don't see why it was wrong. Nobody caught me.
7. But Daddy, I *tried* to call my art teacher Mr. Smith, but he told us to call him Charlie.
8. I don't see why I have to learn grammar. People can understand me when I talk.
9. Why do I need to make good grades? I can always go to college *somewhere* just as long as I graduate.
10. How old were *you* when you started dating?
11. I don't see where smoking marijuana is any worse than getting drunk.
12. Show me *where* the Bible says its wrong.
13. If I lived in some of those poor countries, *I* wouldn't starve. I would get a job.
14. I don't see *why* I have to sweep the floor. It just gets dirty again.
15. I don't think it's fair. I had to do the dishes *last* night.

31

The Tyranny of Interest

"How can he cram his head so full of that worthless stuff and forget something important the next minute?"

The date was February 2, 1983. The teacher was a rookie just out of college, a mere wisp of a girl. The lesson for the day was a class participation drill in the uses of nouns in sentences. Despite what you might think, the students were actually excited about it, and they were doing their best to get things right for the young teacher.

Finally, it was Brad's turn. "Give me," the teacher said, "a sentence using a noun as a direct object."

Almost as if he were seizing an opportunity, Brad answered, "In 1951, Bobby Thompson hit the shot heard round the world." It was a perfect example of the principle and a good sentence, full of poetic allusion. Of course, neither the teacher nor any of the students knew what he was talking about. Since I was the only one in the room old enough to remember or care about such things as New York Giants and Brooklyn Dodgers, his recitation of ancient history went almost unappreciated. But at least he had the opportunity to let his hobby creep into his schoolwork.

Now, this is the same fellow who earlier in the day couldn't remember the capital of North Dakota for a geography test and couldn't spell botany on a science exam. But he knew his baseball. Not only could he tell you the names, clubs, batting averages, and salaries of everyone presently playing, he could go back into the golden years and remember when the enterprise was still a sport.

Actually, the Brads are rather common in junior high. They are not to be confused with the intellectuals. For the most part, they don't care all that much about things like history and science and direct objects. They have simply established themselves as experts on one subject—cars, rock-and-roll music, sports, animals, the Civil War.

Although this kind of intense hobbying can be something of a trial, particularly when you are trying to get the garbage carried out, it is still a rather healthy activity. I would much prefer to see a student interested in baseball instead of one not interested in anything. In fact, I think it is wholesome for parents and teachers to encourage this kind of thing even though the hobby may detract from studying and chores.

Now that I have given you that piece of persuasion, I must admit that I don't really know how to promote hobbies, especially intense ones. People get into them and cherish them for various reasons. Some junior highers seem to follow the lead of their parents or some other close adult, while others tend to rebel against family activities and search for something that is distinctively theirs. Some junior highers respond to direct suggestions, while some prefer to think they have come up with the idea themselves. Some junior highers like to have a hobby with high visibility, while others prefer to keep a low profile.

So from this variety of preferences, we reach one conclusion. Be careful of generalities.

On the other hand, it is important for parents to realize the value of a hobby and to help the junior higher protect it. You're probably more noble and less compulsive than I am, but if Brad were my son, I would have to fight against the urge to punish him through his hobby. "If you miss curfew one more time (or if your grade doesn't come up), I am going to take those baseball cards away from you and put them away for three years."

Of course, that's a foolish statement for a couple of reasons. For one thing, the threat isn't reasonable. Any normal child will say to himself, *Three years. Don't be absurd.* But also, it will be advantageous to both of us for him to keep his interest in that hobby. He will be happier, more active, and more creative going through the junior high years, and we will always have a point of reference.

Besides, I listened to that ball game on the radio, and I am going to get a great deal of pleasure telling Brad about it.

32
A Checklist

In the way of summary, I include this checklist based on the theme of the book, which is that the junior high years are a time of transition for both the child and the parent. The child has to learn to handle changing roles, moods, and body while you as parents have to learn to handle the changing child.

To simplify your task, I have listed some of the changes you should be prepared to expect. Although your junior higher may not encounter all of these and he may encounter some not on the list, at least this list should help minimize the surprises you are going to enjoy during that time when junior highs invade your home.

I. Physical Changes

A. Growth—At this age, body growth is as unpredictable as a hummingbird in flight. We never know when or how much. One year my eighth-grade basketball team traveled to another town where each of my players was between six and twelve inches taller than his opponent. Four years later some of those same boys played again, but this time the athletes were the same size. A short time can make a big difference.

These unpredictable growth spurts concern everybody involved. For one thing, there is often some physical pain involved. Joint problems and shin splints, for example, are common among this age group.

Another problem is awkwardness. When a graceful thirteen-year-old grows six inches in a matter of a few months, he will quite naturally go through some clumsiness before he regains complete control of his arms and legs.

Besides, the dressing problem can be horrendous during this time.

B. Body Hair—Again, this is unpredictable and as such, it becomes something of a symbol of maturity for many junior highers. There is a lot of silent comparison at this age. Your child's need to shave may be more emotional than cosmetic.

C. Voice Changes—To get from childish cries to adult tones one has to go through some squeaks and groans. And those are not always as humorous for the speaker as they are for the listener. When an eighth-grade boy answers the phone and is mistaken for his mother, he is embarrassed. Perhaps this is one reason why junior highers prefer each other's company. They don't have to explain the vocal ups and downs.

D. Sexual Development—With increased sexual power comes increased curiosity and an imperative need for counseling, direction, and understanding.

E. Skin Problems—Regardless of precautions, these are almost inevitable, and they are a source of frustration and embarrassment. Part of being a parent is knowing when to consult a dermatologist.

II. Social Changes

A. Widening Social Circle—For most young people, junior high offers a variety of social opportunities with a variety of people. For many, this variety comes unexpectedly; and it often complicates the role of the parents.

B. Role Changes—Junior high is filled with surprises. Popular people lose their starring roles, and the unknowns often blossom. These changes never come easily for the participants, because they demand that the young person learn a whole new set of emotional responses.

C. Family Relationships—During junior high, your child will need his family identification perhaps more than at any other period in his life, although it may seem as if he is denying it. To younger brothers and sisters, he is a hero. To older siblings, he is a nuisance.

D. Egocentrism—As Charlie Brown's friends huddle to discuss the movie they have just seen, he stands outside and wonders what they are saying about him. The junior higher may often get the idea that he is the center of the conversation, even though he isn't.

III. Emotional Changes

A. The Independent/Dependent Paradox—The junior higher needs adults, but he may not act like it. Most need some external structure although they may fight against it.

B. Extremes—For some unexplained reason (or perhaps for several reasons) the junior higher may pass from one emotion to its opposite at any moment. People in his path may not understand why.

C. Experimentation—Since the junior higher is almost always adjusting to something new—voice, body, social role, or whatever—he has to develop a whole new system of emotional responses. This takes some trial and error (and some extreme reactions at times).

IV. Intellectual Changes

A. Concrete to Abstract—Developmental psychologists tell us that people should move from thinking in concrete, material terms to more abstract thinking between the ages of twelve to fifteen. This change does not come without problems. The junior higher has a great need for consistent, concrete models who will demonstrate in applied action the abstract realities.

B. Demand for Learning Tools—During most of elementary school, students work at developing the basic learning skills of reading, writing, and arithmetic functions. In junior high, they are expected to use those skills to master content.

If a junior higher is deficient in any skill, he will suffer academically and perhaps socially.

Yesterday he came to me
    To talk of grace and justice and grown-up things.
Today he pouted
    Because his basketball had gone flat.

Yesterday we explored the mysteries
    Of work and the world and the working world
    And we peeked into the future to see things fit.

Today he dallied after school
    And forgot the garbage.

Yesterday we dug deep
    Into the sobering joy of love, commitment,
    and permanence.

Today he giggled through the science lesson
    Because his partner was, "Ugh, a girl."

What is this creature
    I have here?
A man too young? A child too old?
    A hero too timid? A coward too bold?

With brave apprehension he gulps and sips
    From the tides of life
    Reaching out for what is to be
    While clutching what has been!

And all the while hating that horrid bump on his chin.